From Sunset to Dawn

From Sunset to Dawn

A Book of Meditations to Help Those in Grief

by

Leslie R. Smith

Christ changes all our sunsets into dawns.
—Clement of Alexandria

ABINGDON PRESS
Nashville • *New York*

FROM SUNSET TO DAWN

Copyright MCMXLIV by Whitmore & Stone

ISBN 0-687-13664-4

Library of Congress Catalog Card Number: 46-4209

MANUFACTURED BY THE PARTHENON PRESS AT
NASHVILLE, TENNESSEE, UNITED STATES OF AMERICA

IN LOVING MEMORY

OF

_____

Whose life with such radiance was lived
that death is but another venture

Foreword

Man foretells afar
The courses of the stars; the very hour
He knows when they shall darken or grow bright;
Yet doth the eclipse of Sorrow and of Death
Come unforewarned.

—WILLIAM CULLEN BRYANT

So death has claimed your loved one. Of course you were not prepared for this separation. One never is. Your adjustment must come during the days ahead, after friends have gone to their homes and to their work. Alone, you must work out your own salvation.

It is for these lonely days that I have written the following meditations, in the hope that they may guide you progressively out of the vale of tears and into the heights of joy. Do not read the book at one sitting. Rather read one brief meditation each day. Carry its truth with you; think upon it, whatever your duties may be, wherever they may lead you.

If only a little comfort comes to one who has suffered, I shall feel fully repaid for my effort in writing.

FROM SUNSET TO DAWN

My garden has roses red,
   My garden has roses white;
But if when the day is sped
   I stand by the gate at night
The fragrance comes, when the day is dead,
From my roses white and my roses red.

The roses of joy are red,
   The roses of pain are white;
But I think, when the day is sped
   And I stand by the gate at night,
I shall know just this, when the day is dead,
That a rose is sweet be it white or red.

—P. C. AINSWORTH

That this may be your experience is my sincere prayer.

LESLIE R. SMITH

Table of Contents

PART I

SOME COMFORTING THOUGHTS TO REMEMBER

PART II

SOME SUGGESTIONS TO FOLLOW

PART III

SOME BLESSINGS TO BE GAINED

A FINAL WORD

SOME COMFORTING THOUGHTS
TO REMEMBER

1. Death Is Natural

In pastures green? Not always; sometimes He
Who knoweth best, in kindness leadeth me
In weary ways, where heavy shadows be—

And by still waters? No, not always so;
Ofttimes the heavy tempests round me blow,
And o'er my soul the waves and billows go.

—Attributed to H. H. Barry

"It is as natural to die as to be born," declared Bacon. All things finally die. Death is the one great certainty. When a child is born into the world, no one can predict whether he will be rich or poor, in what part of the country he will live, what occupation he will follow. Only one thing is certain—one day he will die. Death is natural.

The birds of the air and the beasts of the field,

when their time has come, quietly go away to some peaceful place, and there build their last lair and lie down to die unafraid.

Men ought likewise to look upon death as a natural part of life. When it comes, no bird stops its singing, all life continues to move along oblivious to one's sorrow. At first this seems very cruel. But, on second thought, it reveals the naturalness of the experience.

Every moment marks the passing of someone into the great beyond.

Just before he died, President William R. Harper, of the University of Chicago, was asked by a friend just how he viewed death. The old educator, well aware that he had only a matter of hours to live, remarked with a twinkle in his eye, "As I see death, it does not seem to be nearly so important an event in my career as when I was leaving Yale University and coming here to assume the responsibilities of leadership in the new Chicago University." To him, it was a perfectly natural incident in a long life filled with many greater happenings.

2. Death Is Necessary

Whate'er my God ordains is right;
Here will I take my stand,

DEATH IS NECESSARY

Though sorrow, need, or death make earth
　　For me a desert land.
My Father's care is 'round me there,
　　He holds me that I shall not fall;
And so to Him I leave it all.

　　　　　　　　　　　—S. RODIGAST

Death is necessary. Let us imagine, if we can, just what a tragic state of affairs would exist if nothing and no one had died since the beginning of time. The earth would be cluttered, and life could not continue.

Or let us think of it from the standpoint of the human body. There comes a time when the old shell will no longer sustain the spirit that lives in it. Death is often a true release from pain and suffering. It is necessary to the best interest of each of us.

The Greeks have a legend about Tithonus, to whom the gods granted immortality. They forgot, however, to grant him eternal youth, and he lived on and on, until he was the only one of his age. All his friends had gone. He could not make friends with those who were younger because his body, now wracked with age, could not keep up with them. His life became so miserable that he longed to die. To cast off the old cloak for the new is far more desirable than forever to have to wear the old.

It is only through death that new life can come. What a misfortune it would be if the seed were not

planted in the ground, that it might die and bring
forth new shoots!

> Once, I was but a seed,
> Brown and unlovely too.
> I never knew
> The kindly wind that blew
> To meet my wistful need,
> To make me, in that hour, a living thing
> With dim potential power of blossoming.
>
> And yet, I could not live
> The life I never planned,
> Until a human hand
> Laid hold of me, and taught me
> That Life is given to give,
> That I must die if I would truly be
> The lovely thing the Giver saw in me.
>
> So, in the dark, I died.
> And there and then
> Life found me,
> Loosed the grave-clothes that bound me,
> And let me go,
> That weary earth-stained men
> Might see and know
> How Death is but a doorway to perfection,
> To all the glories of the Resurrection.
>
> —FAY INCHFAWN

DEATH IS NECESSARY

Since death is a natural and necessary part of life, no one ought to be afraid of it. True are the words uttered by William Penn: "Death being the way and condition of Life, we cannot love to live if we cannot bear to die."

As we grow older our attitude toward death becomes more kindly. Beautifully writes one just before he lost his wife:

> We're old folks now, companion,
>   Our heads, they are growing gray;
> But taking the year, all round, my dear,
>   You always will find the May.
> We've had our May my darling,
>   And our roses, long ago;
> And the time of the year is come, my dear,
>   For the silent night and the snow.
>
> And God is God, my darling,
>   Of night as well as of day,
> And we feel and know that we can go
>   Wherever He leads the way.
> Aye! God of the night, my darling—
>   Of the night of death so grim;
> And the gate that from life leads out, good wife,
>   Is the gate that leads to Him!

—Author unknown

3. *The Common Fate*

Sorrow is universal. The experience through which you are now passing comes to everyone at some time. Do not feel you have been singled out to be made miserable. At long last no one is spared. Even the Master wept before the tomb of Lazarus. So will it always be. "Men die, but sorrow never dies," mused Sarah Woolsey. Grief is a part of life.

> There is no flock, however watched and tended,
>   But one dead lamb is there!
> There is no fireside, howsoe'er defended,
>   But has one vacant chair!
>
> —LONGFELLOW

An Eastern legend tells of a woman who lost her only child. In her grief she went to a prophet and begged him to restore the child to her. The old man looked long and understandingly at her, and then tenderly counseled, "Go and bring me a handful of rice from some home where sorrow has not entered, and I shall grant your wish."

The little Oriental mother began her search. Here and there she went; but always the reply to her question was the same. In every dwelling there was an empty chair at the table, a vacant seat before the hearth.

Slowly the sorrow of others touched her sorrowing heart. Soon her sympathy went out to them in their grief. Gradually the waves of her own despair subsided. She found her comfort in the universal presence of weeping.

So may you and I. There are those very close to us whose sorrow we now can understand and appreciate. We should find, if we sought carefully, even in the lives of our enemies enough suffering and sorrow to turn our hostility to compassion.

Sorrow comes to all. No one suffers alone.

> Be still, sad heart! and cease repining;
> Behind the clouds is the sun still shining;
> Thy fate is the common fate of all,
> Into each life some rain must fall,
>   Some days must be dark and dreary.
>
> —LONGFELLOW

4. *Nothing Is Destroyed*

There is no death! The stars go down
  To rise upon some other shore,
And bright in heaven's jeweled crown
  They shine for evermore.

17

FROM SUNSET TO DAWN

There is no death! The forest leaves
　　Convert to life the viewless air;
The rocks disorganize to feed
　　The hungry moss they bear.

There is no death! The dust we tread
　　Shall change beneath the summer showers
To golden grain or mellow fruit
　　Or rainbow-tinted flowers.

And ever near us, though unseen,
　　The dear immortal spirits tread;
For all the boundless universe
　　Is life—there are no dead!

—JOHN L. McCREERY

The Century of Progress exposition in Chicago was opened by a light ray from Arcturus. It took this beam of light forty years to travel from that distant planet. Yet it was not lost; it kept its identity.

But Arcturus is one of the closest stars. Others are thousands of light-years from us. This is to say, it takes thousands of years for their light, traveling 186,000 miles per second, to come to us. Is it not a startling fact that through all this time and space the light is not lost?

Matter is indestructible. It may change its form, but it is not destroyed. We light the wood in our fireplaces, and soon the fire goes out. But the wood is not lost; it has just changed its form into smoke, gas, and ashes. The tree which falls unseen in the forest may decay and rot. But it is not lost. It becomes a part of the rich loam which nourishes other growth.

Likewise, energy continues. It may pass from heat, to light, to motion, to electricity; but it is not lost.

There seems to be a strange law of conservation in the universe. Nothing, not even that which is material, is lost. How can we reason, then, that spiritual qualities will be destroyed? We know that man is greater than the wood which makes up a tree. If that cannot be destroyed, surely neither can he. As it changes its form, so may he do when death comes. This is what Paul seemed to infer when he declared, "Behold, I tell you a mystery: We all shall not sleep, but we shall all be changed."

Influence does not die. This is true whether it be good or bad. It will live on. Ian Maclaren beautifully portrays the power of good influence in the life of young John in *Beside the Bonnie Brier Bush*. Just before his mother died she said to him: "Ye 'ill no forget me, John, I ken that weel, and I'll never forget you. I've loved ye here, and I'll love ye yonder. Th'ill no be an 'oor when I'll no pray for ye, and I'll ken better what to ask than I did here, sae dinna be comfortless. . . . Ye 'ill follow Christ. . . . He 'ill keep ye too, and, John, I'll be watchin' for ye. Ye 'ill no fail me. . . . If God calls ye to the ministry ye 'ill no refuse, an' the first day ye preach in yir ain kirk, speak a gude word

19

for Jesus Christ, an', John, I'll hear ye that day, though ye 'ill no see me, and I'll be satisfied." And John became a minister. His mother's influence lived on through him.

Goodness cannot die. When one stands beside the lifeless form of a saintly person who has been very near and dear to him, something insists that that person is not dead—he was just too good to die. George H. Palmer has expressed this in an unforgettable way in the closing sentence of the biography of his wife, Alice Freeman Palmer: "Though no regrets are proper for the manner of her death, who can contemplate the fact of it and not call the world irrational, if out of deference to a few particles of disordered matter it excludes so fair a spirit."

Personality must continue. It is unreasonable to suppose that just as it is beginning to build something worth while, it should be cut off. Man would be wiser than to permit this. He would not drill deep into the earth until he struck a perennial spring and then after a few bucketfuls of the fresh clear water had been drawn plug the well, and make all his effort useless. Surely God will not let a man mature, learn how to conquer life, just begin to create real value—and then heartlessly cut him off. Our world shows no such insanity in the realm of light, or matter, or energy, or chemistry. We should be insane to expect it in the realm of the spirit. Rather should we hearken to

Emerson, who, after the death of his precious little
five-year-old boy, heard in his poetic soul these words:

> What is excellent,
> As God lives, is permanent;
> Hearts are dust, hearts' loves remain
> Hearts' love will meet thee again.

5. *Continuing Growth*

At twilight when I lean the gunwale o'er
And watch the water turning from the bow,
I sometimes think the best is here and now,
This voyage all, and naught the hidden shore,
Is there no help, and must we make the land?
Shall every sailing in some haven cease?
And must the chain rush out, the anchor strike the sand,
And is there from its fetters no release?
Ah no! our Steersman is forever young,
And with much gladness sails beneath the stars;
Our ship is old, yet still her sails are hung
Like eager wings upon the steady spars.
Then tell me not of havens for the soul
Where tides can never come, nor storms molest!
My sailing-spirit seeks no sheltered goal,
Naught is more sad than safety; life is best
When every day brings danger for delight,

21

And each new, solemn night
Engulfs our whitening wake within the whole.

—EVELYN UNDERHILL

Mark Twain is reported to have said that he certainly didn't want to go to heaven if it meant that he would have to sit on a cloud and strum a harp through all eternity.

In one of Whittier's poems an old monk poetically expresses a similar feeling. He belonged to the order of the Brothers of Mercy. Naturally, his life had been filled with hardships and toil. Now he lay dying. His confessor, as he sat by the bed, tried to console him with the assurance that soon he would sit in a white robe, wearing a golden crown, in the beautiful land of tomorrow. But the thought brought no comfort to the old recluse. He mumbled:

> Miserable me!
> I am too poor for such grand company;
> The crown would be too heavy for this gray
> Old head; and God forgive me if I say
> It would be hard to sit there night and day,
> Like an image in the Tribune, doing naught
> With these hard hands, that all my life have wrought,
> Not for bread only, but for pity's sake.
>
> .   .   .   .
>   Will death change me so
> That I shall sit among the lazy saints,

Turning a deaf ear to the sore complaints
Of souls that suffer?

Most of us feel the same. We would rather think of heaven as a place where we can further develop the personalities which we have begun to unfold here on earth.

God doesn't bring shoots of greenery just above the surface of the earth to nip them in the bud before they have the chance to bring forth their fruit. This is not the way of nature. The normal thing is for them to grow and to unfold that which is latent within them. This is not unlike what we may expect for man. It would be a cruel and a thoughtless universe—which ours is not—that would permit man to begin to unfold the beauties and strength of personality which lie within him, and then cut him off.

Creative energy declares that one cannot go backward—he must go forward. All of life is expressive of this truth. It is a progression through age. We have no right to suppose that death ends all. It rather opens the way to more progress.

We came into this world, and immediately the process of growth continued just where it had left off before our birth. When we pass into the next world, we may expect the same continuation of growth.

Within the hearts of us there is always a deep dissatisfaction. We are the most unsatisfied beings in the world. Always the best within us cries out for greater expression. We feel we were made for high and holy things. Every other creature, without this urge in him toward higher things, is limited to growth here on earth. But we are greater than the beasts of the field. We know no limit.

Bishop McConnell tells of being called to the bedside of one of his professors. Almost jubilantly the former teacher told the Bishop that he knew the end was very near but he also knew that five minutes after he had reached the other shore he would be seeking out one of his scholarly opponents that they might continue the debates on the subjects on which they disagreed while they taught together here on earth.

Near a shady wall a rose once grew,
   Budded and blossomed in God's free light,
Watered and fed by morning dew,
   Shedding its sweetness day and night.

As it grew and blossomed fair and tall,
   Slowly rising to loftier height,
It came to a crevice in the wall,
   Through which there shone a beam of light.

Onward it crept with added strength,
   With never a thought of fear or pride;
It followed the light through the crevice's length
   And unfolded itself on the other side.

24

The light, the dew, the broadening view
  Were found the same as they were before;
And it lost itself in beauties new,
  Breathing its fragrance more and more.

Shall claim of death cause us to grieve
  And make our courage faint and fall?
Nay! let us faith and hope receive;
  The rose still grows beyond the wall;

Scattering fragrance far and wide,
  Just as it did in days of yore,
Just as it did on the other side,
  Just as it will forever more.

—A. L. Frink

6. *Your Home Is Waiting*

One day in his eightieth year John Quincy Adams was tottering down a Boston street. He was accosted by a friend who said, "And how is John Quincy Adams today?"

The former president of the United States replied graciously, "Thank you, John Quincy Adams is well, sir, quite well, I thank you. But the house in which he lives at present is becoming dilapidated. It is tottering upon its foundations. Time and the seasons have nearly destroyed it. Its roof is pretty well worn out, its walls are much shattered, and it trembles with every wind. The old tenement is becoming almost uninhabitable, and I think John Quincy Adams will have to move out of it soon; but he himself is quite well, sir, quite well." And with this the venerable statesman, leaning heavily upon his cane, moved slowly down the street.

John Quincy Adams had the same assurance which we all have. He knew that "if the earthly house of our tabernacle be dissolved, we have a building from God, a house not made with hands, eternal, in the heavens."

If we fear or question the future, we have not come to a true realization of Jesus' counsel, "Let not your heart be troubled. . . . I go to prepare a place for you. . . . . that where I am, there ye may be also."

We had nothing to do with our coming into this world, yet when we arrived there was a place all prepared for us by the loving care and thought of our parents and friends. Can we not expect the same when we depart from this life?

It helps both him who dies and him who is left to believe that death is just a home-going. Several years ago, while living in Nebraska, I accepted a call to a church in Southern California. My wife's and my home had always been in the Middle West. Our parents, still living, resided there. We were now to go two thousand miles away. It was hard for all concerned. Then one day a letter came from my new

Board of Elders saying that they had secured a house for us and that our little home in the West would be waiting for us. Because the way had been prepared it was easier for our family to depart—and it was much easier for our parents to let us go. So it is with dying.

Will Rogers in his crude but understanding way, showed this to be the way he looked at death. Charlie Russell, a Montana cowboy, artist, writer, and close friend, asked Mr. Rogers to write the foreword for his book *Trails Plowed Under.* But the author died before the book was published, so as a foreword Will Rogers wrote this letter to him:

There aint much news here to tell you, You know the big Boss gent sent a hand over and got you so quick Charley, But I guess He needed a good man pretty bad, I hear they been a working short-handed over there pretty much all the time, I guess its hard for Him to get hold of good men, they are just getting scarce everywhere . . . I bet you hadent been up there three days till you had out your old Pencial and was drawing something funny about some of their old punchers . . . I bet you Mark Twain and old Bill Nye, and Whitcomb Riley and a whole bunch of those old Joshers was just a waiting for you to pop in with all the latest ones, What kind of a Bird is Washington and Jefferson I bet they are regula fellows when you meet em aint they?, most big men are. I would like to see the bunch that is gathered around you the first time you tell the one about putting the limburger cheese in the old Nestors Whiskers.

Dont tell that Charley till you get Lincoln around you, he would love that, I bet you and him kinder throw in togeather when you get well acquainted, Darn it when I get to thinking about all them Top Hands up there, If I could just hold a Horse wrangling job with em, I wouldent mind following that wagon myself.

You will run onto my old Dad up there Charley, For he was a real Cowhand and bet he is running a wagon, and you will pop into some well kept ranch house over under some cool shady trees and you will be asked to have dinner, and it will be the best one you ever had in your life, Well, when you are thanking the women folks, You just tell the sweet looking little old lady that you knew her boy back on an outfit you used to rep for, and tell the daughters that you knew their brother, and if you see a cute looking little rascal running around there kiss him for me. Well cant write you any more Charley dam paper is all wet, It must be raining in this old bunkhouse.

Course we are all just a hanging on here as long as we can. I dont know why we hate to go, we know its better there, Mayby its because we havent done anything that will live after we are gone.

from your old friend,

WILL

In like faith Robert Freeman, the late minister of the Pasadena Presbyterian Church, poured out his poetic soul in his poem "The Other Room":

No, not cold beneath the grasses,
  Not close-walled within the tomb;
Rather, in my Father's mansion,
  Living in another room.

Living, like the one who loves me,
  Like yon child with cheeks abloom,
Out of sight, at desk or school book,
  Busy in another room.

Nearer than the youth whom fortune
  Beckons where the strange lands loom;
Just behind the hanging curtain,
  Serving in another room.

Shall I doubt my Father's mercy?
  Shall I think of death as doom,
Or the stepping o'er the threshold
  To a bigger, brighter room?

Shall I blame my Father's wisdom?
  Shall I sit enswathed in gloom,
When I know my love is happy,
  Waiting in the other room?

7. *An Eternal Tomorrow*

When all is done, say not my day is o'er,
And that through night I seek a dimmer shore;

Say rather that my morn has just begun,—
I greet the dawn and not a setting sun,
    When all is done.

—Paul Laurence Dunbar

When the great minds of all ages have focused
their thought on death, they all seem to have come
to the same conclusion—that death is not an end but
a beginning, that after Good Friday comes Easter,
that we rightly look forward to an eternal tomorrow.
Thus muses Victor Hugo: "When I go down to the
grave I must say like so many others, 'I have finished
my day's work.' But I cannot say, 'I have finished
my life.' My day's work will begin the next morning. The tomb is not a blind alley. It is a thorough-
fare. It closes in the twilight to open in the dawn."

Others have tersely spoken the same truth: Seneca,
"Death is the birthday of immortality"; Robert
Browning, "Never say that I am dead"; Ludwig
Beethoven, "I shall hear now"; Goethe, "Open the
shutters and let in more light"; Dwight L. Moody,
"Earth is receding; heaven is approaching; God is
calling me"; Douglas Jerrold, "I feel as one who is
waiting and waited for"; Sir Walter Scott, "I feel
as if I were to be myself again."

Through symbolic acts we learn that in their deepest feeling men have always believed that to die was
simply to enter into a brighter day. The old Egyptian
mummy cases have the face of the deceased person

depicted upon them with eyes wide open, suggesting life. The Truscans, long before Christ's coming, made their tombs face the west, the land of the setting sun. But after the Resurrection they built them to face the east, significant of a new day. Ellen Terry, a noted English actress of a few decades ago, had her casket made in the form of a cradle.

It seems trite to say that men depart so that they may arrive. Yet this is true of the journey of life and death. Our faith leads us to hope for the morrow. Dr. R. J. Campbell used to tell the story of a little girl who was accustomed always to express her good night in the same words. Simply she said, "Good night; I shall see you again in the morning." And then death stole in prematurely for one so bright and gay as she. But with childlike trust, yet knowing she could not get well, she called her daddy to her, slipped her arms around his neck, and whispered faintly, "Good night, Daddy; I shall see you in the morning."

Death is not eternal; it is the morning which breaks thereafter that continues. Despite the darkness of this hour, we need to remember that life carries on, even through death. Nature affirms our faith by reminding us that spring comes on forever.

> There must be rough, cold weather,
>   And winds and rains so wild;

Not all good things together,
  Come to us here, my child.

So, when some dear joy loses
  Its beauteous summer glow
Think how the roots of the roses
  Are kept alive in the snow.
                              —ALICE CARY

8. *An Eternal Fellowship*

And so for me there is no sting of death,
  And so the grave has lost its victory.
It is but crossing—with abated breath
  And white, set face—a little strip of sea
To find the loved ones waiting on the shore,
  More beautiful, more precious than before.
                              —ELLA WHEELER WILCOX

One of the most helpful thoughts which has ever come to me is that those who die simply go to another home where there are many who await their coming.

I am standing upon the seashore; a ship at my side spreads her white sails to the morning breeze and starts for the blue ocean.

She is an object of beauty and strength, and I stand and watch her until—at length—she hangs like a speck of white cloud just where the sea and sky come down to mingle with each other.

Then someone at my side says, "There! She's gone." Gone where? Gone from my sight—that is all.

She is just as large in mast and hull and spar as she was when she left my side and just as able to bear her load of living freight to the place of destination.

Her diminished size is in me, not in her; and just at the moment when someone at my side says, "There! She's gone," there are other eyes watching her coming and other voices ready to take up the glad shout, "There she comes!"

And that is dying.

—Author unknown

Not only does it help me to feel that my loved one has gone to a happy reunion, but my own attitude is greatly sweetened as I feel that I am not only waiting but being waited for. If I knew that in six months I should have to die, this thought would be a solace to me.

Said a saintly lady to me some days before she passed away, "I'm really getting a little anxious to go on the great journey. I have tried to console my daughter by telling her that I now have more of my family on the other side than I shall be leaving here. I am looking forward to being with them."

> All that tread
> The globe are but a handful to the tribes
> That slumber in its bosom.
>
> —WILLIAM CULLEN BRYANT

To meditate upon the fellowship of the great which one joins when he steps over into the other world, while almost overpowering, is nonetheless thrilling.

> Yet not to thine eternal resting-place
> Shalt thou retire alone—nor couldst thou wish
> Couch more magnificent. Thou shalt lie down
> With patriarchs of the infant world—with kings,
> The powerful of the earth—the wise, the good,
> Fair forms, and hoary seers of ages past,
> All in one mighty sepulchre.
>
> —WILLIAM CULLEN BRYANT

The story is told of a school inspector who visited a little one-room schoolhouse in the western part of our country. Jokingly he asked the one teacher, "And do you have any staff to assist you in your work?"

Quickly the schoolmaster replied, "Indeed I do. Plato, Aristotle, Milton, Browning, Shakespeare— these, and many more, are on my staff."

What a glorious group from which to learn! How unutterable would be the joy of associating with them! This can be our hope.

Call me not dead when I, indeed, have gone
Into the company of the ever-living
High and most glorious poets! Let thanksgiving
Rather be made. Say: "He at last hath won
Rest and release, converse supreme and wise,
Music and song and light of immortal faces;
To-day, perhaps wandering in starry places,
He hath met Keats, and known him by his eyes.
To-morrow (who can say!) Shakespeare may pass,
And our lost friend just catch one syllable
Of that three-centuried wit that kept so well;
Or Milton; or Dante, looking on the grass
Thinking of Beatrice, and listening still
To chanted hymns that sound from the heavenly hill."

—RICHARD WATSON GILDER

9. *Present Though Unseen*

Far off thou art, but ever nigh;
 I have thee still, and I rejoice;
 I prosper, circled with thy voice;
I shall not lose thee tho' I die.

—TENNYSON

Those who have suffered grief testify that after the
first shock of separation has quieted, they come to
feel their loved one is closer to them than ever before.

35

Death breaks down all barriers of time and space. Thus Stanton, in his funeral eulogy of Abraham Lincoln, could declare, "Now he belongs to the ages." Had Christ continued to live upon this earth he could never have been the universal companion he now is. He would always have been limited to some locality where his physical person dwelt. Thus he might not always have been present with us in the hour when we needed him most. Much the same is true of the one you have lost. You no longer feel you are parted for a single moment of the day. You are always together. Thus speaks Frederick Hosmer in "My Dead":

> I cannot think of them as dead
> Who walk with me no more;
> Along the path of life I tread
> They have but gone before.

> The Father's house is mansioned fair
> Beyond my vision dim;
> All souls are His, and here or there
> Are living unto Him.

> And still their silent ministry
> Within my heart hath place,
> As when they on earth walked with me
> And met me face to face.

Their lives are made forever mine;
　What they to me have been,
Hath left henceforth its seal and sign
　Engraven deep within.

Mine are they by an ownership
　Nor time nor death can free;
For God hath given to Love to keep
　Its own eternally.

I remember meeting a lady two years after I had buried her husband. She came toward me with arms outstretched and eyes tear filled. A flood of memories coursed through the minds of each of us. She hastened to assure me, "I never felt closer to my husband than now. I used to think of him as being about his work, away from me, and I was alone. But now we are together all the while, in every thought and deed. . . . The other day someone referred to me as a 'widow.' I was shocked for a moment that anyone should consider me that." Indeed they are not gone who have passed beyond our clasp, for they softly walk in our thoughts by day and in our dreams by night.

Then seek to find comfort. Go about your daily duties in the glorious realization that the one you love is very near to you. Do not go too often to his grave and thereby limit him to a mound of earth in some particular geographic location. If you do sometimes place flowers there, you should have the assurance, "He is not here."

A friend whose husband died placed his picture on her piano, and beside it she ever kept a single fresh flower. He was always with her, as your loved one can be with you. You can have a small sacred shrine in your home and in your heart.

10. Eternity Is Now

Death is only an old door
  Set in a garden wall;
On gentle hinges it gives, at dusk
  When the thrushes call.

Along the lintel are green leaves,
  Beyond the light lies still;
Very willing and weary feet
  Go over that sill.

There is nothing to trouble any heart;
  Nothing to hurt at all.
Death is only a quiet door
  In an old wall.

—Nancy Byrd Turner

To look upon death as the end is to plunge ourselves into the awful despair of utter hopelessness. To look upon it as the beginning of another life is to separate ourselves from our loved ones and to postpone the comfort which rightly should come. But to think of the present as a part of eternity (what else can eternity mean?) is to realize that death is no more than stepping into another room. It is just an old door which opens upon a beautiful garden.

Eternal life, then, is not a gift to be bestowed upon us in some strange hereafter; it is rather a present possession. Thus Jesus, speaking in the present tense, declares, "He that believeth hath eternal life," and "This is life eternal, that they should know thee the only true God."

Someone made the penetrating observation that we cannot have heaven in prospect until we have heaven in possession. Theodore Mundo requested that his epitaph read, "Here endeth the first lesson." You and I, who are alive, are in the midst of eternity.

> There is no Death! What seems so is transition;
>   This life of mortal breath
> Is but a suburb of the life elysian,
>   Whose portal we call Death.
>
> —LONGFELLOW

Herein lies a real challenge for us. We are partakers of eternity with the loved ones who have gone ahead of us. They have been graduated to a higher grade, while we are still in the elementary section. The more perfect a child's physical development before his birth, the more perfect is his life after birth. So it is with immortality. To assure having much in common when again we meet, we need to number our days that we may apply our hearts unto wisdom.

So live, that when thy summons comes to join
The innumerable caravan, that moves
To that mysterious realm, where each shall take
His chamber in the silent halls of death,
Thou go not, like the quarry-slave at night,
Scourged to his dungeon, but, sustained and soothed
By an unfaltering trust, approach thy grave,
Like one who wraps the drapery of his couch
About him, and lies down to pleasant dreams.

—WILLIAM CULLEN BRYANT

11. He Is Just Away

I cannot say, and I will not say
That he is dead.—He is just away!

With a cheery smile, and a wave of the hand,
He has wandered into an unknown land,

40

HE IS JUST AWAY

And left us dreaming how very fair
It needs must be, since he lingers there.

And you—O you, who the wildest yearn
For the old-time step and the glad return,—

Think of him faring on, as dear
In the love of There as the love of Here.

Think of him still as the same, I say:
He is not dead—he is just away!

—JAMES WHITCOMB RILEY

To think of one's dead as just being away is to find true comfort. Of course we should like to have our loved ones always with us, or to be always with them. But this is not possible—as all parents know. Although they love their children, they must see them leave the family home. When a lad goes away to college, his parents revel in the joy they know he is having. Much the same attitude can be taken toward death. Wrote the loving parent of a young lad who had just died, "I hardly know how to tell you—and I have not told you before simply because I did not have the heart to do so—that our dear boy entered his new life last month. Only the thought of his rich and wonderful experiences in these first days of his new life consoles us, or in any way makes up for the loss we feel in his absence."

Surely we should not weep if some friend or relative

had the good fortune to go to a locality where he could better himself. We should rather wish him the best and speed him on his way. If we did otherwise, we should reveal our own selfishness. And yet many resent, even more than they mourn, the going of a loved one.

It is better by far to consider that the one who has died has just preceded us to a place where we shall soon go. Declared Benjamin Franklin, "Our friend and we were invited abroad on a party of pleasure, which is to last forever. His chair was ready first, and he has gone before us. We could not all start conveniently together; and why should you and I be grieved at this, since we are soon to follow, and know where to find him?"

> Say not the boy is dead, but rather say
> He's but a little farther on the way,
> Impatient sooner to behold the view—
> At the next turning you may see it, too.
> Say he's a child again, early to bed,
> On night's soft pillow fain to lay his head.
> Say he is off to track the mountain stream,
> And lingers by the side in boyish dream.
> Say by immortal waters now at rest,
> He clasps a thousand memories to his breast.
> Say to his wondering quests wise angels, smiling,
> Tell the true story of the world's beguiling.
> Say on heroic task his soul is thrilling
> Where noble dream hath noble deeds fulfilling.

Say that he feasts with comrades tried and true,
But in his heart the banquet waits for you.
Say in the Presence, at a gentle word
He shows the wound-marks to his wounded Lord.
Say never he is dead, but rather say,
He's but a little farther on the way.

—Author unknown

12. *Death Is Like Sleep*

As a fond mother, when the day is o'er,
  Leads by the hand her little child to bed,
  Half willing, half reluctant to be led
  And leave his broken playthings on the floor,
Still gazing at them through the open door,
  Nor wholly reassured and comforted
  By promises of others in their stead,
  Which, though more splendid, may not please him
    more;
So nature deals with us, and takes away
  Our playthings one by one, and by the hand
  Leads us to rest so gently, that we go
Scarce knowing if we wish to go or stay,
  Being too full of sleep to understand
  How far the unknown transcends the what we know.

—Longfellow

43

How delicious sleep can be! Can you think of anything more desirable than to lie down and rest after a hard day's labor? Death, declares the Master, is like that. Our bodies are worn out—in fact, cannot serve us longer. We simply lie down to rest.

Within the memory of all of us is the sense of complete peace which came when, as children, mother tucked us into bed, where we snuggled so warm and comfortable, and gave us a good night kiss. We knew that on the morrow we should awaken, refreshed and happy, to find her love continuing right where her good night kiss had left off. How like death!

> So I looked up to God,
> And while I held my breath
> I saw Him slowly nod,
> And knew—as I had never known aught else,
> With certainty sublime and passionate
> Shot through and through
> With sheer unutterable bliss—
> I knew
> There was no death but this,
> God's kiss,
> And then the waking to an Everlasting Love.
>
> —G. A. STUDDERT KENNEDY

13. *Whichever Way the Wind*

⟨∾⟩

Just as a mother carries her helpless babe safe in her arms, away from the threatening flames, so God upholds us in time of danger. There is a painting in the National Gallery in London which wonderfully portrays this truth. It is a study of the crucifixion. The figure on the cross stands out with startling distinctness against a dark background. At first glance this seems to be all of the picture. But as one looks intently at it he sees a figure back of the cross, whose arms, extended, hold up the Master. Underneath him, in his hour of need, are the everlasting arms.

Whatever our experience, we have this same assurance, the same that came to Moses of old—God's love and care continue.

> I know not what the future hath
>   Of marvel or surprise,
> Assured alone that life and death
>   His mercy underlies.
>
> I know not where His islands lift
>   Their fronded palms in air;
> I only know I cannot drift
>   Beyond His love and care.

—WHITTIER

45

Charles H. Spurgeon was one day calling on some of his country parishioners when he noticed a strange weather vane on top of one of the barns. Across it were the words, "God is love." Mr. Spurgeon inquired of his friend, "Do you mean God's love changes every time the wind blows?"

"No," replied the man, "I mean God loves us no matter which way the wind blows."

This is a welcome truth. Sorrow does not shut out God. He is here now, willing to uphold us. We can never get away from his love and care. In fact, we are always in the middle of it. Nothing can harm or hurt us there. God will not forsake us, because we are his children.

A minister was summering on an island in a small lake in northern Minnesota. An old French-Canadian and his wife acted as caretakers for his summer camp. One day he asked his woodsman friend why he and his wife, since they were both nearly eighty years of age, did not go for the winter to Bemidge, where the climate was much milder. The old man replied, "No can do." When pressed for a reason, he took the minister along a path through the woods to a small clearing, at the center of which was a mound of earth with fresh flowers on it. As they neared the grave, the crude old woodsman removed his cap as he simply explained, "We no can leave ze baby." For more than forty years this couple had braved the rigorous winters of this little island because on it was invested all that they really possessed. In like manner, God will not forsake this world, for he invested his only begotten Son in it. And that One declared that we too are children of the Eternal. He will not leave us. Underneath, upholding us, are his arms.

God has cared for us very well until now. He prepared loving hands to receive us when we came to this earth. Many are the blessings which have daily come to us from his hand. It is folly to suppose he will forget us now. And it must be right to predict that he will have a place already prepared for our loved ones "over there."

In time, we shall come to see this sorrow in its right light. Only as the days pass will we understand just why it should have come into our lives. One day we may be able to affirm the question,

> Is my gloom, after all,
> Shade of His hand, outstretched caressingly?
>
> —Francis Thompson

A four-year-old boy lay sick of a fever; his father reclined near him in the dark. Now and then the lad would half wake, call to his father, hear the reassuring voice, and slip again into sleep. All who grieve are fever flushed and troubled. Rest and peace come with the assurance of God's presence. He is here now. He enfolds you in his love. He knows your grief and understands. You have no need to fear.

A little easeful sighing,
    And restful turning round,
And I too, on Thy love relying,
    Shall slumber sound.
—William Canton

14. The Blessing of Night

The night is kind, oh, very kind,
    In darkness to immerse
One little world and then reveal
    A boundless universe.
—Alice Crowell Hoffman

A small child who saw the stars for the first time was greatly impressed and intrigued by them. Childlike, she had many questions. Were they there all the time? Why couldn't you see them during the day? Couldn't you see them until it got dark? Her mother replied, "Yes, their beauty is hidden all through the day. You can see them only at night. Aren't they lovely?" And then she added, "Darkness is always beautiful if we will only look up at the stars instead of into the corners."

How true! If we will just look up at the stars! They tell us that night is the most joyous part of the day. It is the time of homecoming after a hard day's work. We step out of the limited interest of business associates and friends into the boundless love of home and family. In this happy fellowship we relax after the strain of a busy day. Night is the time for rest and for sleep.

So it is with death. It is life's night. It is a glorious homecoming. It is a reunion with those who have gone before. It is rest from labor. It is simply to lie back in the Everlasting Arms.

But the stars tell us still more. They remind us that they are part of a vast universe which moves in perfect rhythm and orderliness upheld by a dependable law. There is something eternal and sure about them, upon which we can rely.

A number of years ago another planet was discovered. Twenty-five years before it was found, Dr. Lowell, a Yale astronomer, had charted on the map of the heavens a spot where, some day, another planet would be sighted. He insisted that such a body existed because of the way the other planets and the sun behaved. Accepting the dependability of the law of the universe, he could make no other explanation of their behavior. The universe did not let him down; in due time the new planet swam into view.

Neither will it let us down. The Power which fixes

the course of the heavenly bodies is far more interested in us than he is in them. This is natural, is it not? We can judge from our own attitudes. A man is far more valuable than an automobile. It is not egotism to believe that God is more concerned about men than he is about the whirling spheres of flaming rock which form the stars. Jesus insisted that a sparrow cannot fall but that the heavenly Father knows it, that the very hairs of our head are numbered. Indeed we can trust our loved one to such a Power! What comfort the stars do bring!

And they show us the folly of fear. As children we may have been afraid of the dark. But now we know it holds no harm for us. It is childish to fear death. No monster grim is it which steals upon us to do us harm. It is a part of the great plan which keeps the stars in the sky.

In Maeterlinck's *Blue Bird* there is a scene which I can never forget. Do you remember how the children had stolen into the churchyard at the eerie hour of midnight? As they stood in the little cemetery there, they questioned each other in scarcely audible whispers, "Where are the dead?" Suddenly there came a great peal of thunder which almost frightened them out of their wits. Everything around them was covered with a heavy mist. They were so afraid they could not move. Then the mist began to clear away. It rose as a curtain from the ground. And lo, the tombstones were all gone! Only beautiful white flowers were in their stead. The dawn was already breaking. "Where are the dead?" they had asked—and now the boy shouted back to his sister, who stood trembling at his side, what that night had taught them, "There are no dead."

Here, then, are the blessings of night: it is the most reassuring time of all the day, it reveals to us the unfaltering care of an Eternal One, and so it takes away all fear. Darkness—even the darkness of death—is always beautiful if we will only look up at the stars.

15. Death Is a Release

Youth may look upon death as an unwelcome thing, but age or suffering knows it is often a blessed release. There are times when the physical becomes so depleted that it can no longer contain the spiritual. Hence that which is eternal leaves this earthly abode and enters that realm where pain and suffering cannot go. Most of us cannot wish that he who suffered much should be brought back to that agony. In time of grief we ought to pin our thought not upon our loss but rather upon the release which has come to the one who has left us.

Naïvely, but beautifully, a small girl summarized for her Sunday school teacher the story of Enoch. She said, "Enoch used to go on long walks with God. One day they walked farther than usual, and God said, 'Enoch, you are tired. Come into my house and rest.'"

This is a true picture of death. It is a release from pain and fatigue. It is rest for those who are weary. So much of a release is it, and so beautiful does it appear, that those who have been near death seem unanimous in expressing a feeling of regret that they should be snatched from it back to life. Thus writes A. C. Benson: "Once in a moment of perfect health, in the Alps, I came very near to death indeed in a crevasse. I was rescued only just in time, after swimming faintly away in my expiring breath. I certainly had no sense of fear; and stranger still, on recovering, my first thought was not of relief, but of unwillingness to be recalled to life. It seemed all over and done with, and I seemed caught back from something more real than life."

Death is a release not only from suffering but also from the worldly, limited life on earth. Paul sensed this when he said, "Then shall I know fully even as also I was fully known."

It is as though the one who has left you has grown so tall that his head pierces the clouds. The glory revealed beyond is now his possession.

DEATH IS A RELEASE

Mrs. Gatty in her *Parables of Nature* has a lovely story of a water lily which lifts its head above the waves that reflect its golden crown and satin folds of whiteness. But she reminds one as he looks at this lovely creation of nature not to forget that if he should follow the stem down, down through the water, he would find its roots buried in the slime and mire. The root and the blossom cannot be separated. Neither can our sojourn here and "over there." As the water lily knew not its fullest release until it unfolded above the water into the glorious light of the sun, so man does not know his fulfillment, or release, until he passes beyond the gate of the finite into the realm of the infinite. Although the following verse may belittle life too much, this can be excused since it was written in the style and thought of more than three hundred years ago. It does rightly picture the blessing of freedom which death can bring.

Death is a port whereby we pass to joy:
Life is a lake which drowneth all in pain:
Death is so dear, it ceaseth all annoy;
Life is so leud, that all it yields is vain:
And as, by life, to bondage man is brought:
E'en so likewise by death is freedom wrought.

—Author unknown

16. It Is Best

ᴄᴡᴠᴏ

Precious thought, my Father knoweth,
  In His love I rest;
For whate'er my Father doeth
  Must be always best.
                              —Author unknown

When you can look upon the departure of your
loved one and muse, "I know it is best," you have
made the turn toward the renewal of your spirit.

Of course if this one has been suffering intense
physical pain, or has lived so far beyond his allotted
time that his body is no longer a fit temple for his
soul, it is quite easy to be reconciled to his going.
But even if the truth that it was best is less evident,
we still can believe that all is well.

Many things could have happened which would
have proved to be much worse than death. To be
paralyzed for life, to be incapacitated mentally, to become a burden to someone—these would have been
far worse. Indeed, it is well that both he and you
have been spared these things.

And then, who can tell what trials might have
lurked in the future, what temptations or sins might
have proved too powerful? Selfishly we wanted to

keep him. With our incomplete knowledge we do wrong to insist.

A tiny moth tried to invade my study one summer night. Attracted by the light, he seemed to think only of getting in to it. And so he beat his body vainly against the screen. Had he succeeded in entering my room, he no doubt would have starved or burned to death. But his limited knowledge did not let him sense this. So it is with us. We ought not cry against the fate which has befallen us. There are many things worse than death which might have overtaken our loved one if he had lived.

> And you shall shortly know that lengthened breath
>   Is not the sweetest gift God sends His friend,
> And that, sometimes, the sable pall of death
>   Conceals the fairest boon His love can send.

—Mary L. R. Smith

PART II

SOME SUGGESTIONS TO FOLLOW

17. Accept the Fact

∽✵∾

What was the answer of God's love
Of old, when in the olive grove
In anguish-sweat His own Son lay,
And prayed, "O God, take this cup away"?
Did God take from Him then the cup?
No, child, His Son must drink it up.

—HENRIK IBSEN

When a bird is flying for pleasure, it drifts with the wind. But if a tempest is blowing it turns around and heads directly into the storm. No longer does it flap its wings. It simply soars. Because of its complete surrender to the gale it is borne higher and higher until once again, above the storm, it can fly freely as it will.

Those who fly airplanes have learned this lesson from the birds. One of their first rules is to turn the ship toward the wind. We who would pilot our lives through the storm of grief must learn to do the same. We have to face our sorrow; we cannot run away from it. No good is gained if we cry out, or rebel against it; we have to surrender to it. And then a strange thing happens. What had seemed unbearable finally gets beneath us and bears us up, ever upward into the realm where God's comfort can make itself known. Our very suffering has become the means of our spiritual ascent.

Katherine Mansfield had to face the fact of her own death while yet very young. Early in her brilliant career she was stricken with the dread disease tuberculosis. To the astonishment of all her friends she continued her writing for several years when it seemed that her weakness and pain must surely overcome her. But always she proved superior to them. What was the secret of her power? Perhaps these lines from her *Journal,* written shortly before her death, give a clue: "I do not want to die without leaving a record of my belief that suffering can be overcome. For I do believe it. What must one do? There is no question of what is called 'passing beyond it.' Make it a part of life."

Just so, our first step toward the comfort we covet and the adjustment to life which we must make will come only after we have unequivocally surrendered to the finality of the fact of death, when we have fully accepted the certainty of our grief. Any other attitude will only magnify our misery.

Have you been crying out, "Why, oh why, has this

come to me? What have I done to be so treated?"—
only to receive no answer but the empty echo of your
own voice? That hollow reply can only deepen your
loneliness.

Have you rebelled against God, have you doubted
his justice and good will, because your loved one has
slipped away from you? This is only beating your
head against a stone wall. It cannot restore to life the
one whom you mourn.

Have you tried to evade the whole problem of
death and sorrow? This is folly. There is no need of
pretending. The inevitable fact will finally overtake
you, and in your exhaustion you will give way to
rank bitterness.

Have you felt sorry for yourself? This adds only
another pain to the one you already bear.

Frankly, there is nothing to do but to accept the
fact and to surrender to its reality.

This does not mean that we give ourselves over to
a fatalistic resignation. Rather we face the real facts
of our condition, we make them a part of our lives,
we give them a place in the pattern of our future
activity.

Some travelers were returning from the Orient
with a tablecloth of priceless, handwoven linen. As
they were proudly showing it to some of their friends
on the boat an inkwell was accidentally overturned on
it. Fortunately a young and talented Oriental was

among those who saw the catastrophe. He asked if he might have the cloth for the rest of the journey. It was given to him. On the day before the ship docked he returned the cloth to its owner. Her delight was great when she saw in the place of the ugly blot of ink a beautifully embroidered rose. This, with other roses, now formed a colorful border to this lovely piece of linen and made it still more priceless. Despair, rebellion, evasion, or self-pity would never have made this feat possible. Only as the fact was accepted and made a part of life was it possible for comfort to come and an adjustment to be made. God does not take away our grief. He lifts us above it.

> I like the man who faces what he must
> With step triumphant and a heart of cheer;
> Who fights the daily battle without fear;
> Sees his hopes fail, yet keeps unfaltering trust
> That God is God,—that somehow, true and just
> His plans work out for mortals; not a tear
> Is shed when fortune, which the world holds dear,
> Falls from his grasp—better, with love, a crust
> Than loving in dishonor; envies not,
> Nor loses faith in man; but does his best,
> Nor ever murmurs at his humbler lot;
> But, with a smile and words of hope, gives zest
> To every toiler. He alone is great
> Who by a life heroic conquers fate.
>
> —SARAH K. BOLTON

18. Step by Step

〜〰〜

If but one message I may leave behind,
One single word of courage for my kind,
It would be this—Oh, brother, sister, friend,
Whatever life may bring, what God may send,
No matter whether clouds lift soon or late,
Take heart and wait.

Despair may tangle darkly at your feet,
Your faith be dimmed, and hope, once cool and sweet,
Be lost; but suddenly above a hill,
A heavenly lamp, set on a heavenly sill
Will shine for you and point the way to go,
How well I know.

For I have waited through the dark, and I
Have seen a star rise in the blackest sky
Repeatedly—it has not failed me yet.
And I have learned God never will forget
To light His lamp. If we but wait for it,
It will be lit.

—GRACE NOLL CROWELL

They that wait for Jehovah shall renew their strength.
—Isaiah 40:31

This is a difficult lesson to learn. Yet it is a never-failing truth. One of the greatest curses of sorrow can be the impatience which accompanies it. Many people think the wound should be healed immediately. It cannot be. It takes time. If we can surrender to the fact and believe that through it God will teach us many things, gradually, step by step, we shall find comfort.

You dare not worry about the long years of loneliness which lie ahead. Rather know that with each day sufficient strength will come to carry you through.

This must have been the truth which John H. Newman felt when he wrote in his best-known hymn:

> Lead, kindly Light, amid the encircling gloom,
> Lead Thou me on!
> The night is dark, and I am far from home;
> Lead Thou me on!
> Keep Thou my feet; I do not ask to see
> The distant scene, one step enough for me.

19. Count Your Blessings

> All are not taken: there are left behind
> Living beloveds, tender looks to bring
> And make the daylight still a happy thing,
> And tender voices to make soft the wind.
>
> —ELIZABETH BARRETT BROWNING

61

The grateful person can always be comforted. He is not selfish in his grief. He refuses to look just at the sorrowful parting. He insists on seeing about him the many blessings of God's hand. Would you be comforted? Then develop the grateful spirit.

Each morning, when you waken, name over ten things for which you are grateful. Perhaps your baby girl is brushing aside the tears as they drop from your eyes. No doubt some friend has meant much to you. If you have a home and are well cared for, how happy you should be. There are thousands of things which will come to your mind.

You might well reinforce your thought with passages of scripture. They abound in a listing of blessings. Here are only a few: Third John, chapter 2 (blessings of health); Mark 5:19 (of home); Psalm 65:9-13 (of plenty); First Samuel 18:1-4 (of friendship); Second Timothy 1:7 (of sanity); Ecclesiastes 5:12 (of work).

Be grateful for the time you had your loved one with you. This is a much more healthful and helpful attitude than rebellion against his going.

> God lent him to me for my very own,
> Let me become his father, me alone!
> Gave him to me not for an hour—for years!
> ('Tis gratefulness gleams in my eyes, not tears!)
> No joy that fathers know but it was mine
> In fathering that laddie strong and fine.

COUNT YOUR BLESSINGS

Time after time I said: " 'Tis but a dream;
I shall awake to find things only seem
Grand as they are!" Yet still he lingered on
Till year on sweeter year had come and gone.
My heart is filled forever with a song
Because God let me have my lad so long.

He was my own until I fully knew
And never could forget how deep and true
A father's love for his own son may be.
It drew me nearer God Himself; for He
Has loved His Son. (These are but grateful tears
That he was with me all those happy years!)

—STRICKLAND GILLILAN

Thank God for what this sorrow is doing for you.
Nothing comes to you that cannot be used for the en-
larging of your life and character. No experience is a
loss. Perhaps you have been frivolous, thoughtless,
taking all good things too much for granted. But now
that you have known the depths of suffering, all life
has taken on new light. You hardly know yourself.
Your thoughts seem to come from elsewhere. Be glad
of your sorrow.

Is it raining, little flower?
    Be glad of rain!
Too much sun would wither thee;
    'Twill shine again.
The clouds are very black, 'tis true;
    But just behind them shines the blue.

Art thou weary, tender heart?
  Be glad of pain!
In sorrow sweetest virtues grow,
  As flowers in rain.
God watches, and thou wilt have sun,
  When clouds their perfect work have done.
                                    —LUCY LARCOM

Of course, your greatest consolation is that God still lives, that life goes on. It is a great sentence in just two words that the Mohammedan always engraves on the tombstone of his departed: God Remains." Knowing this, we cannot but be grateful.

But one thing more: *do something* about this gratitude. Make it active. Go beyond mere words. Anne Lindbergh declares in *Listen! the Wind:* "One can never thank people—at least not by piling gratitude on top of them like heavy American Beauty roses. One can never pay in gratitude; one can only pay 'in kind' somewhere else in life. Unconsciously, perhaps."

The natives in Uganda, Africa, when they meet a friend on the path, say not "Good day," as we do, but in their native tongue declare, "I thank you." This is the attitude you must have. Your blessings are all around you. Keep your eyes open to your mercies, counsels Robert Louis Stevenson, for "the man who forgets to be thankful has fallen asleep in life." Count your blessings.

Breathe the following prayer over and over. Repeat

the third stanza until you believe its truth. And God
will be very near.

> My God, I thank Thee who hast made
>   The Earth so bright;
> So full of splendor and of joy,
>   Beauty and light;
> So many glorious things are here,
>   Noble and right!
>
> I thank Thee, too, That Thou hast made
>   Joy to abound;
> So many gentle thoughts and deeds
>   Circling us round,
> That in the darkest spot of Earth
>   Some love is found.
>
> I thank Thee *more* that all our joy
>   Is touched with pain;
> That shadows fall on brighest hours;
>   That thorns remain;
> So that Earth's bliss may be our guide,
>   And not our chain.
>
> I thank Thee, Lord, that here our souls,
>   Though amply blest,
> Can never find, although they seek,
>   A perfect rest,—
> Nor ever shall, until they lean
>   On Jesus' breast!

> —ADELAIDE A. PROCTER

20. Serve Others

When all our hopes are gone,
'Tis well our hands must still keep toiling on
  For others' sake;
For strength to bear is found in duty done,
  And he is blest indeed who learns to make
  The joy of others cure his own heartache.

—Author unknown

Sorrow brings with it a grave danger. How often those in sorrow neglect the duties they owe to those who are living while they selfishly indulge in mourning for the dead. They succumb to the temptations of suffering. They withdraw themselves from the life of men. They sit alone, keep silence, nurse their grief. In my ministry I have known those who gave up all church work, who refused even to attend the services of their church, who would not see anyone's need but their own. Because they refused to do the things which would bring comfort, their souls became dead seas filled with brine and salt, barren and desolate.

Such people wonder why their grief becomes so unbearable. They ought to recall the words of John Ruskin: "Every duty we omit obscures some truth we should have known." He who withdraws himself will never know the comfort which comes for serving other people. Said a woman whose only son I had buried, "When it seems I just can't stand my grief any longer, I bake a cake for someone who isn't expecting it." This is a homely philosophy, but entirely sound.

Grief sometimes makes us forget our importance to God's plan. If we fail to help those around us, the chances are they will not be helped. To suppose we are not necessary to the high service of philanthropy is to accuse God of an extravagance in his creation. Spurgeon once exploded in contradition to this attitude, "God doesn't have time to make nobodies!" Indeed he does not. There is work today which we must do even though we may have buried our dearest one only yesterday.

To help another today is to save regret tomorrow. Life at best is very uncertain. No doubt all of us have at some time bemoaned the fact that we did not help another who was in need. And then suddenly he left us. The kindness was still in our possession. He did not know. Bitter words, and cankerous to the soul are these: "I should have, but didn't; and now it is too late."

Many have found a victorious way out of their grief by lending a helping hand to others. The lovely French countess of La Garaye rode forth to the hunt one morning with her gay company. Of a sudden she was thrown from her horse and crippled for life. One of lesser breeding might have lost herself in remorse, but not this royal lady. With the help of her understanding husband she transformed their castle into a home for incurables like herself. They found new joy in serving those who needed the type of help which they, because of their experience, could give better than anyone else.

John Watson, author of *Beside the Bonnie Brier Bush,* used to counsel folk to be kind to one another, for most of us are fighting a hard battle. And he seemed to live by the truth of his own preaching. For long after the people of a former charge had forgotten what he said from the pulpit they still remembered the man who spent long hours pouring out wonderful stories to hot, restless little folk too ill to look at pictures, sick of all their toys, or peevish and fretted by their crumby beds.

The association of John Bright and his wife was particularly close and beautiful. With her going all hope and joy left his life. His friends became worried; they feared for his mind. Then the visit of one touched a chord which responded. Let the noted Englishman tell his own story:

Mr. Cobden called upon me as his friend, and addressed me, as you might suppose, with words of condolence. After a time he looked up and said, "There are thousands of houses in England at this moment where wives, mothers, and children are dying of hunger. Now," he said, "when the first paroxysm of your grief is past I would advise you to come with me, and we will never rest till the Corn Law is repealed." I accepted his invitation. I knew that the description he had given of the homes of thousands was not an exaggerated description. I felt in my conscience that there was a work which someone must do, and therefore I accepted his invitation, and from that time we never ceased to labor hard on behalf of the resolution which we had made.

In serving others he found comfort. You and I can do the same.

21. Comforted to Comfort

Hast thou borne a secret sorrow
   In thy lonely breast?
Take to thee thy sorrowing brother
   For a guest.

Share with him thy bread of blessing
   Sorrow's burden share;
When thy heart enfolds a brother,
   God is there.
          —THEODORE C. WILLIAMS

Blessed be the God and Father of our Lord Jesus Christ, the Father of mercies and God of all comfort;

who comforteth us in all our affliction, that we may be able to comfort them that are in any affliction, through the comfort wherewith we ourselves are comforted of God.

—II Corinthians 1:3-4

Paul seemed to possess much of the knowledge of modern psychology even though the word was unknown in his day. Intuitively he knew that if one received comfort in the hour of sorrow and selfishly prized the healing which had come to his heart, without any effort to comfort others, he would soon lose the very thing in which he rejoiced. We are comforted, not just to rise above our own tribulation, but that we may help a brother. Thus George Matheson counsels: "Thou canst not cure thine own sorrow by nursing it; the longer it is nursed, the more inveterate it grows. It will be harder for thee to go out tomorrow than it is today; it will be harder still the day after. Thou canst not cure thy sorrow by nursing it; but thou canst cure it by nursing another's sorrow."

It appears that God comforts us not to make us comfortable, but to make us comforters. Indeed, we can never completely understand our sorrow unless we seek an answer to this question, What good to others is meant to come through me, by this? Then

> Ask God to give thee skill
> In comfort's art,

That thou may'st consecrated be
 And set apart
Unto a life of sympathy,
For heavy is the weight of ill
 In every heart;
And comforters are needed much
 Of Christlike touch.

—A. E. HAMILTON

Go now to your telephone, to your desk, or on a personal call, and comfort another who needs your help. A greater joy than you have yet known will come to your heart.

22. Do Not Bear Your Grief Alone

. . . casting all your anxiety upon him, because he careth
 for you.

—I Peter 5:7

O Lord, how happy should we be
If we could cast our care on Thee,
 If we from self could rest;
And feel at heart that One above,
In perfect wisdom, perfect love,
 Is working for the best.

—J. AUSTICE

71

Cast thy burden on the Lord—this is exactly what God intends for us to do. He has never meant that we should carry it entirely by ourselves. To do so is sheer egotism. It always leads to despair. He would have us remember that we are not alone, that he still cares for us, that he has not forgotten us or the world. To realize this is to cut our grief in half. He who never senses that there are certain times when we come to the end of our human strength and need divine help is shutting out his chief source of comfort.

"I can't!" despairingly I cried!
    This gentle whisper sounded at my side,
"Of course not, child, thou wast not fashioned so,
    But I, thy Father, CAN and WILL. I know
Thy weakness, all thy longing see,
    And I am always strong to strengthen thee.
                                        —MARY O'HARA

And yet it is difficult to let go our burden. Why? Perhaps we reason, "Only a weakling would try to drag God into his situation." This is to forget God's nature. He is a Father. If my lad is trying to move an object too large for him, I do not hesitate to answer his call for help. Neither does God. Thus to seek the help of another is not weakness; it is common sense, born of an understanding of the purpose of God and the magnitude of our burden.

A motorist stopped in the north country to pick up

an old man who was trudging along the highway with an exceedingly heavy pack upon his shoulders. He noticed, as they rode, that the man continued to carry his burden. He counseled him to lay it in the seat. Then came this astonishing reply, "But, sir, you are so kind to give me a ride that I don't want to make you carry my bundle, too." Foolish, indeed, yet no more so than the erroneous feeling that we should be weak if we cast our burden upon the Eternal.

We may hesitate because of our pride. We are hurt that anything so tragic should happen to us. But to face up frankly to this attitude is to abhor it.

Or it may be we enjoy our grief. When one is controlled by a deep mood he often resents any attempt to lift him out of it. We can see this in children. We ought not let it characterize our sorrow. No less a one than Robert Louis Stevenson admits that when he was particularly sorrowful he would go to a cemetery and sit on a tombstone to imbibe more grief.

Perhaps we have not yet completely accepted the fact which has confronted us. And so we continue to pit our will against that of the Father in heaven. We feel our plans have been thwarted. We do not submit to God's way. We try to force him to fulfill our desires. We are slow to surrender our little wills to his greater wisdom.

There is One who stands beside you now whose example you may dare to follow. On the cross he was unable to bear his agony alone. At first he cried out in his despair, "My God, my God, why has thou forsaken me?" And then he said what all of us who are sorrowing must finally say, "Father, into thy hands I commend my spirit."

Can you say that now, meaning it?

Cast all your care upon him, for he careth for you.

23. *The Comfort of Friends*

For even when we were come into Macedonia our flesh had no relief, but we were afflicted on every side; without were fightings, within were fears. Nevertheless he that comforteth the lowly, even God, comforted us by the coming of Titus; and not by his coming only, but also by the comfort wherewith he was comforted in you, while he told us your longing, your mourning, your zeal for me; so that I rejoiced yet more.

—II Corinthians 7:5-7

One of the greatest comforts which can come in time of grief is the presence of those who love us. Over and over again those who are borne down in sorrow have said to me, "I didn't know I had so many friends." Just to be assured that one is not alone, that there are those who understand and care, and in a measure grieve with us, is to find real consolation.

Paul evidently needed just such comfort in his trial. He writes that he was greatly comforted by the coming of his close friend and student, Titus. We should not wonder that we crave the same help. It is natural. And friends, no matter how poorly they may be able to express their thoughts in words, are eager to extend that help. In such an hour we sense the deeper truth of the hymn:

> We share our mutual woes,
> Our mutual burdens bear,
> And often for each other flows
> The sympathizing tear.

We find healing particularly with those who have suffered a like sorrow to our own. Understanding comes out of like experience. One should not feel his grief is different from or greater than anyone's. Let those who have suffered speak with you and tell you of their own triumph. When you cry out in despair, "How can I stand this? It is more than I can bear," then listen to their counsel: "How can you bear this? I can tell you, for I have borne it." You are not alone. Others have come through the experience triumphantly. You can do the same.

> Have courage, soul of mine;
> The path that you must keep

Is long and lone and steep.
But many thousand feet
Have passed this way before;
All through the vanished years
These stones were wet with tears.
If others knew this road,
And bore their heavy load,
If others went this way,
You, too, can bear the heat
And burden of the day,
You, too, can bear dark night
Until the morning light.
If others passed this way
Have courage, soul of mine.

—MARY E. ROCK

Believe me when I say it is through those who have triumphed over sorrow that

God stooping shows sufficient of his light
For us i' the dark to rise by.

—BROWNING

In *My Lady of the Chimney Corner* Alexander Irvine has a touching passage in which he shows how God does come to us through the love and sympathy of our friends. Eliza is grief stricken over the sudden death of her lad Henry. Anna, her close friend, is with her. Eliza is almost irrational in her sorrow. Finally Anna induces her to kneel down and ask God to lay his hand on her head. As Eliza breathes this prayer, Anna very gently lays her hand on the stricken mother's head.

"Oh, oh, oh, He's done it, Anna, He's done it, glory be t' God, He's done it!"

"Rise up, dear," Anna said, "an' tell me about it."

"There was a nice feelin' went down through me, Anna, an' th' han' was just like yours."

"The han' was mine," replied Anna gently, "but it was God's hand, too." "Listen, dear," Anna said, "God's arm is not shortened. He takes a han' wherever He can find it and just diz what He likes wi' it. Sometimes He takes a bishop's and lays it on a child's head in benediction, then He takes the han' of a docthur t' relieve pain, th' han' of a mother t' guide her chile, an' sometimes He takes th' han' of an aul craither like me t' give a bit o' comfort to a neighbor. But they're all han's touch't by His Spirit and His Spirit is everwhere lukin' for han's t' use."

And we need not confine ourselves to our immediate friends. The history of the ages is filled with stories of those who have suffered just as you are suffering and who have come through the experience victoriously. Not the least of these is the Master. Even he was not spared. We are assured that through his stripes, we are healed. Christina Rossetti, sensing this truth, penned the following:

> Christ's heart was wrung for me; if mine is sore,
> And if my feet are weary, His have bled;

He had no place wherein to lay His head;
If I am burdened, He was burdened more;
The cup I drink, He drank of long before;
He felt the unuttered anguish which I dread;
He hungered, who the world's refreshment bore.
If grief be such a looking-glass as shows
Christ's face and man's in some sort made alike
Then grief is pleasure with a subtle taste;
Wherefore should any fret or faint or haste?
Grief is not grievous to a soul that knows
Christ comes—and listens for that hour to strike.

Then take an active attitude toward your friends. Do not sit and wait for them to do all things for you. When the first few days are over, and they have returned to their duties, do not bemoan the fact that they have left you. When you feel the need of their friendship, tell them, and they will gladly respond. Finally, thank God for friends. They are, indeed, a providential gift.

Oh, ray of light, my friend!
    When sorrow's gloom made life so drear,
Then comfort sweet thy words did lend,
    As if Christ spake, "Be of good cheer!"

Oh, rock of strength, my friend!
    When shifting sands beneath my feet
And changing scenes my steps attend,
    Thy truth and constancy are sweet.

I clasp thy hand, my friend!
  Thank God that thou art here;
I am not worthy He should send
  To me a gift so dear.

                      —Author unknown

24. Sing

Be like a bird
That pausing in her flight
Awhile on boughs too slight,
  Feels them give way
Beneath her and yet sings,
Knowing that she hath wings.

                      —VICTOR HUGO

A member of a church choir into whose life a great sorrow had come confided to his pastor that he felt he could never sing again. What a mistaken idea, for sorrow could bring even greater feeling to his music! And yet his attitude is that of many. Perhaps you have felt the beauty of harmony has slipped forever from your grasp. This ought not to be. If one refuses to sing in his grief, he is shutting off one of the sure sources of comfort. The children of Israel sang their songs in the land of their captivity. They returned again to Zion. There is a direct relation.

Many people do not go to church after the death of a loved one because they "can't stand the music." And the longer they stay away, the more difficult it is to return. This does not seem to be God's plan.

Song is buoyant. We need our spirits lifted. We deliberately imbibe grief when we refuse to take part in singing. It would prove a healing balm if only we would permit it.

There is a story of thirty-six thousand songbirds that were brought from across the sea. Most of them were canaries. They sat in their tiny cages, calm, with heads tucked away beneath their wings, for the sea was calm and life was easy. But on the third day from shore a great storm broke. The ship rocked to and fro. The fury of the gale and the heaving of the sea gave the officers concern for the safety of the ship. The children were frightened and began to cry. And then one of the birds began to sing. Soon all thirty-six thousand of them were singing at the top of their voices. The more the boat rocked the more loudly they sang. Fear left the faintest heart as all aboard listened to this magnificent bird symphony.

Song in the hour of storm will do the same for us. It is not sacrilegious to sing in our sorrow; it is using a God-given restorative.

> Don't let the song go out of your life,
> Though it chance sometimes to flow

In a minor strain; it will blend again
  With the major tone you know.

What though shadows rise to obscure life's skies,
  And hide for a time the sun;
The sooner they'll lift and reveal the rift,
  If you let the melody run.

Don't let the song go out of your life,
  Though the voice may have lost its trill;
Though the tremulous note may die in your throat,
  Let it sing in your spirit still.

Don't let the song go out of your life:
  Let it ring in the soul while here;
And when you go hence, 'twill follow you thence,
  And live on in another sphere.

                —KATE STILES

25. The Value of Work

When sorrow all your heart would ask
We need not shun our daily task,
  And hide ourselves for calm;
The herbs we seek to heal our woe
Familiar by our pathway grow,
  Our common air is balm.

                —JOHN KEBLE

There is an old Latin poet who, attempting to describe the punishments of the lower world, makes one of the heaviest of them consist of a man's being condemned to do nothing. Such a state of inactivity could produce real suffering. Even though we recognize this, yet we often add the burden of inactivity to that of our sorrow, thus deepening our grief—when to take up our duties and to pursue them would lessen our agony.

> Art thou dejected? Is thy mind o'ercast?
> Amid her fair ones, thou the fairest choose,
> To chase thy gloom.—Go, fix some weighty truth,
> Chain down some passion; do some generous good;
> Teach ignorance to see, or grief to smile;
> Correct thy friend; befriend thy greatest foe;
> Or with warm heart, and confidence divine,
> Spring up, and lay strong hold on Him who made thee.
> —EDWARD YOUNG

If we do shirk our duties at such a time we shall only add a sense of guilt to our sorrow, and this is devastating. Often he who has been the most conscientious in his work finds it most difficult to return to it after the death of a loved one. But his conscience will constantly whip him if he fails to do the things he should.

Not only this, but to shirk our task is to defeat the will of God. Each of us has a role to play in his divine plan; if we fail, then a chord in the Higher Harmony fails. We might well heed the truth which George Eliot causes Stradivari, the old violin maker, to say:

> If my hand slacked
> I should rob God—since He is the fullest good—
> Leaving a blank instead of violins.
> He could not make
> Antonio Stradivari's violins
> Without Antonio.

Did not Robert Browning, when the flower of his life died, throw himself into his writing as never before? Goethe's mother said of her son that when he had a grief he put it into a poem and so forgot it. David Livingstone, the explorer missionary to Africa, when he laid the body of his wife to rest in the heart of that dark continent felt he would just as soon die too. But note what his biographer says: "For such comfort as could be obtained in these dark days, he turned again to his work." And in his *Journal* the explorer himself says: "The sweat of one's brow is no longer a curse; it proves a tonic."

We marveled that during the siege of Leningrad the people of that city continued to clean their streets and paint their houses. Perhaps we were wont to say, "What a waste of time and effort!" Not so; their agony and grief were relieved by their activity.

So he who would find his way out of his grief should attack his work with a zest which he never had before. It is absolutely necessary to set one's hands to something that will absorb his whole attention. Work was given to us as a great benefaction. Let us not turn our backs on it in the hour of our greatest need of it.

26. Read Your Bible

I opened the old, old Bible,
    And looked at a page of Psalms,
Till the wintry sea of my troubles
    Was soothed as by summer calms;
For the words that have helped so many,
    And the ages have made more dear,
Seemed new in their power to comfort,
    As they brought me their word of cheer.

                —Author unknown

When Sir Walter Scott lay dying he asked for "The Book"; and, on being questioned as to what book, he replied, "Need you ask? There is but one." This has been the testimony of many people throughout the years since it was written. *There is but one Book.*

The Book has inspired the greatest productions of music, the most famed masterpieces of painting, the finest works of literature. It likewise is an unfailing source of comfort for those in sorrow, as you will discover if you read the following selections: John, chapters 11, 14, 17, 20; Romans, chapter 8; First Corinthians, chapter 15; Second Corinthians, chapters 4, 5; and Revelation, chapters 7, 21, 22.

The Book contains a great reservoir of biography. Whatever your particular sorrow or trial you can find its counterpart in the holy pages of Scripture. As does no other book, the Bible traces the story of such conflict through all of its stages to victory. You can find there a technique for meeting and overcoming grief.

The Book takes your thought away from the immediate and helps you to see the necessity of a long-range look, if you would grasp the whole truth. It helps you to realize that the sorrow of this moment, like that of Good Friday, is but temporary when seen in its right relationship to the rest of life.

The Book brings a new calm and peace to your mind. Many bear witness to its power. Hear Charlotte Brontë's confession in a letter to Miss Ellen Nussey on February 20, 1837: "Last Sunday I took up my Bible in a gloomy frame of mind. I began to read; a feeling stole over me such as I had not known for many long years—a sweet, placid sensation like those that I remember used to visit me when I was a little child. I thought of my own Ellen. I wished she might have been near me that I might have told her how happy I was, how bright and glorious the pages of God's holy word seemed to me."

85

27. *The Power of Prayer*

⟨᷎⟩

"On your knees, sir! You are safe here only on your knees," shouted the guide as he pulled an inexperienced mountain climber to the ground. The party had just completed the dangerous ascent of the Weisshorn. One of them, anxious to see over the top of the peak and not aware that the gale always blowing there would sweep him over the cliff, had thoughtlessly jumped to his feet. Only the quick action of the guide saved him. In that place of danger he was safe only on his knees. In like manner, we are safe only on our knees in time of sorrow. Otherwise we will be dashed to pieces by the gale of our grief.

We need the quiet moments of prayer because of the healing power which their silence brings.

> With silence only as their benediction,
>   God's angels come;
> Where, in the shadow of a great affliction
>   The soul sits dumb.
>
> —Author unknown

While it is necessary to carry on the activities of our life, we must balance these with periods of silence. Such silence will give us a sense of being not alone in our grief as we think of the many others who are going through like trial to ours, and offer up prayers for them.

Through our meditation it may become clear that the experience of this grief was necessary for us to find a larger fulfillment of life. A blacksmith who had accepted the Christian way seemed to have one difficulty after another. A friend jokingly observed, "Everything seems to be going wrong since you became a Christian, doesn't it?"

But the blacksmith was quick with his reply: "See that scrap iron over there? It isn't worth much. But do you see this carriage spring which I have been hammering unmercifully for hours? I have been putting it back and forth from the fire into cold water and then hammering it some more. Now it is worth four hundred times as much as that pile of scrap iron. I believe God will make me worth far more because of the experiences through which I am going than would be possible if I did not have to face them." Such a conclusion could not come from one's own will. It is only as a person surrenders to a Higher Will that be comes to see the possibilities of his suffering.

Just as physical exercise strengthens the body, so the exercise of prayer strengthens the spirit. Both the medical and psychological professions declare that there is no power which can bring greater calm and more steadying influence than the habit of religious meditation and prayer. This is true because in such an hour one sees life not from his own narrow point of view but from God's perspective.

Thus it was that Dr. Philipp Melanchthon declared, "Trouble and perplexities drive us to prayer, and prayer drives away trouble and perplexity."

> O soul of mine, in grief's dark hour,
> Or when lower ways offer place and power,
> If thou wouldst be always strong and sane,
> Come thou apart to the hill again.
>
> There lay down life at the Master's feet,
> To take it again with strength replete;
> There calmed will be the stress and strain,
> And forward we'll leap to share his pain,
> As we go to the hill again.
>
> —E. STANLEY JONES

28. *This Night Is for Sleep*

> In peace will I both lay me down and sleep;
> For thou, Jehovah, alone makest me dwell in safety.
>
> —Psalm 4:8

God made the night for sleep. He does not intend for us to toss feverishly and wakefully upon our beds. He does not want us to pace our room in purposeless fretting. It is not his will that we sit and dumbly stare into the darkness. God made this night for sleep!

If we use the night as he would have us, we shall awake tomorrow refreshed. Its healing balm will have done its work. If we debase it with care, worry, and tears, our morrow will break dull and cold. Surrender to sleep if you would find rest and comfort.

We were at the seashore. The tide was out. Our boat lay high and dry on the beach. We wanted to launch it. With all our might we pushed, and tugged, and pulled. With every minute of effort we saw the keel plow deeper and deeper into the sand. Exhausted, we gave up the task. Then the tide came flooding in. Soon it bore the boat upon its breast. What our struggle had failed to achieve, our waiting had accomplished.

There are times when our effort, either physical or mental, is vain. Wise is the soul that learns this truth. If tonight is filled with worry, care, anxiety, and sorrow, we shall awake tomorrow exhausted. With the flood tide of his healing sleep God will restore our troubled spirits. He is waiting to uphold us in his everlasting arms. He does not demand that we come to him. He waits for us to come freely. We must surrender of our own choice.

Repeat over and over, nestling into his arms as you

recline upon your bed, "Father, thy love upholds me
I thank thee for this night and for my sleep. Amen."

Be still and sleep, my soul!
   Now gentle-footed night,
In softly shadowed stole,
   Holds all the day from sight.

Why shouldst thou lie and stare
   Against the dark, and toss,
And live again thy care,
   Thine agony and loss?

'Twas given thee to live,
   And thou hast lived it all:
Let that suffice, nor give
   One thought what may befall.

Thou hast no need to wake,
   Thou art no sentinel;
Love all the care will take,
   And Wisdom watcheth well.

Weep not, think not, but rest!
   The stars in silence roll;
On the world's mother-breast,
   Be still and sleep, my soul!

—EDWARD ROWLAND SILL

29. *Trust God*

∽✺∾

A lonely track, perchance a darkened sky,
A mist of tears, and only God knows why—
Is He not worth our trust the voyage through,
He who has not failed us—hitherto?

—MARY GORGES

To be comforted you must trust completely in the
goodness and faithfulness of the Eternal. To do otherwise is to thwart the coming of help to your troubled
mind. Can you believe that God knows best, and
then rest in that belief?

An English minister tells of how he sat one evening with a father and mother beside the bed of their
little child who was near death. He talked with the
parents about life and death and the hope of immortality. Before he offered prayer he questioned,
"What shall we ask God to do?" There was a moment's silence and then the father very simply and
trustingly replied, "We would not dare to decide.
Leave it to him."

Can you do the same? Can you feel that God has
planned wisely and well? To question or to rebel is to
doubt God's wisdom and faithfulness. Trust your
loved ones to him. He is better able to care for them
than you are.

91

A man had suffered almost every conceivable trial in life. It seemed he could not stand another blow. His one salvation had been his little girl whom he dearly loved. And then the awful climax—she died. There was no light in the sky for him. He determined he must follow her. He went to the London Bridge and was ready to cast himself down into the waters beneath, when suddenly the thought struck him, "God is far better able to care for her than I am. Why should I be acting this way? Why should I doubt his mercy?"

The difficulty is we usually judge our Father's love by our condition of pain or sorrow. We should rather judge our earthly condition of pain or sorrow by the Father's love. To a dyspeptic the whole world appears in sordid colors. One has to look upon the world from the standpoint of an eternal plan to catch its true meaning and significance. One needs to look up and to trust.

In one of his books Stevenson tells of a crashing storm at sea. So great was the fury of it that the pilot had to be lashed to his wheel. One of the passengers, who despaired of the outcome, crept up to the deck. Just then the pilot turned and smiled. Reassured and trusting now, she went back to her cabin. So does help come to us if we look away from our grief to the God of love in whom we trust.

TRUST GOD

Under the ever-changing clouds of doubt,
    When others cry,
The stars, if stars there were,
    Are quenched and out!
To him, uplooking to the hills for aid,
    Appear at need displayed,
Gaps in the low-hung gloom and bright in air,
    Orion, or the Bear.

—COVENTRY PATMORE

We should never feel that we must know all the answers to all our questions. Trust is not trust if we know all. God does not expect us to understand all the ways of life any more than we expect our children to understand all our demands upon them. We ask only that they place their trust in our judgment. He asks the same.

A stranger asked a village boy where such and such a town was. The lad replied simply, "I do not know, but there is the path." You do not have to see your destination. One step at a time is enough. As you trust and follow you will find.

Cast thy burden on the Lord,
Only lean upon his word;
Thou shalt soon have cause to bless
His eternal faithfulness.

—Author unknown

30. *Christus Consolator*

∽✺∾

When some belovèd voice that was to you
Both sound and sweetness faileth suddenly,
And silence against which you dare not cry
Aches round you like a strong disease and new,
What hope? what help? what music will undo
That silence to your sense? Not friendship's sigh;
Not reason's subtle count: not melody
Of viols, nor of pipes that Faunus blew;
Not songs of poets, nor of nightingales
Whose hearts leap upward through the cypress-trees
To the clear moon; nor yet the spheric laws
Self-chanted, nor the angels' sweet All hails,
Met in the smile of God: nay, none of these.
Speak THOU, availing Christ! and fill this pause.

—ELIZABETH BARRETT BROWNING

To believe in the Christ and his power over death
is to find a sure comfort. All the other things which
have been mentioned in this section—friends, literature, and the like—cannot bring the sense of peace
which he can. Because he had power over death, we
believe he will give this power to those who follow
him. This is worth remembering.

In the hour of grief we would do well occasionally
to take our thought away from our loved one and to
think of the Master of men, his promise of eternal

life and of his continuing presence. We do not have to bear our grief alone.

The setting of a well-known English artist's masterpiece, "The Comforter," is a squalid room with an iron bedstead and a straight backed chair, the only pieces of furniture. Upon the bed is the lifeless form of a young woman. A wedding ring on the hand which lies on top of the counterpane tells that the man who sits with head bowed in grief by her side is her young husband. Through an open window the crowd can be seen going to and fro in the street, completely oblivious to the tragedy being enacted in that room. But the young man, as he sits there in his anguish, is not alone. Beside him, with one hand on his shoulder, is the filmy figure of the Presence. Underneath the picture are the words, "And lo, I am with you always."

Upon hearing of the death of Lazarus, Jesus went immediately to the Bethany home of his friends. Martha ran to meet him and cried, "Lord, if thou hadst been here, my brother had not died." Jesus comforted her, assured her that he was the resurrection and the life, that if anyone would believe in him he could not die, that Lazarus was not dead but alive. He comes to you in your hour of sorrow, with the same message. Just as he made all things right for Martha and Mary, so can he for you.

Lewis Carroll once wrote a letter to the children

who loved "Alice." In it he described a child awakening from a frightful dream to find a mother's hand drawing aside the curtains and letting in the sunshine of the spring morning. And he goes on to suggest that death is like that—just the awakening to a new day to behold with your own eyes the Sun of Righeousness.

"Let not your heart be troubled. . . . I go to prepare a place . . . that where I am, there ye may be also." "Whosoever liveth and believeth on me shall never die."

Part III

SOME BLESSINGS TO BE GAINED

31. *The Gift of Opposites*

They tell me I must bruise the rose's leaf,
Ere I can keep and use its fragrance brief.
They tell me I must break the skylark's heart,
Ere cage song will make the silent start.
They tell me love must bleed, and friendship weep
Ere in my sorest need I touch that deep.
Must it be always so with precious things,
Must they be bruised, and go with beaten wings?
Ah, yes! by crushing days, by caging nights, by scar
Of thorns and stony ways, these blessings are.
—Author unknown

Life is composed of opposites: daylight and dark, waking and sleeping, good and bad, health and sickness, pleasure and pain, joy and sorrow. It is through the experience of these opposites that we learn. They are the great disciplinarians of life. "There is always a note of pathos," said Bishop Charles L. Slattery, "in the most joyous music; tears are always locked in the happiest smiles; the poems or dramas of love which

97

reveal the highest bliss always include tragedy." To get the full range and capacity of the organ one must play upon the black keys as well as the white.

> Joy and woe are woven fine,
> A clothing for the soul divine:
> Under every grief and pine
> Runs a joy with silken twine.
>
> —WILLIAM BLAKE

One who has always been blessed with good health scarcely appreciates how fortunate he is. It is the one who has suffered an illness who knows the exhilaration of healthfulness. He will never know the height of true joy who has not the capacity for deepest grief. Music cannot come from a violin while the strings are loose. They must be stretched—no doubt would cry out in pain if they could. This very sorrow can deepen your capacity for joy. One scarcely can appreciate the value of life until he is shocked by its brevity and uncertainty.

The opposites of life make human service and sympathy possible, and keep alive the other worth-while qualities of life and character.

> If none were sick and none were sad,
>   What service could we render?
> I think if we were always glad,
>   We scarcely could be tender.

THE GIFT OF OPPOSITES

Did our beloved never need
   Our patient ministration,
Earth would grow cold, and miss, indeed,
   Its sweetest consolation.

If sorrow never claimed our heart,
   And every wish were granted,
Patience would die, and hope depart—
   Life would be disenchanted.

                          —Author unknown

Sameness ever robs life of challenge and interest. A semitropic climate, where it is never very cold nor very hot, produces a lackadaisical attitude toward life. The shade is most refreshing when one has been exposed to the burning sun. Water is most enjoyed when one is quite overcome with thirst. A life without hardship or struggle would be the death of character. Even sorrow has its place.

If all the skies were sunshine
   Our faces would be fain
To feel once more upon them
   The cooling plash of rain.

If all the world were music,
   Our hearts would often long
For one sweet strain of silence,
   To break the endless song.

If life were always merry,
Our souls would seek relief,
And rest from weary laughter
In the quiet arms of grief.

—Henry van Dyke

32. The Gift of Character

I walked a mile with Pleasure;
She chattered all the way,
But left me none the wiser
For all she had to say.

I walked a mile with Sorrow
And ne'er a word said she;
But oh, the things I learned from her
When Sorrow walked with me!

—R. B. Hamilton

Sorrow can either make or break you. Which will it be? It can make you either better or bitter. Which do you choose to let it do?

Many people turn against life because of their grief. They spurn the help of those who would lift them out of their despondency. They withdraw more and more into themselves, where they continue, in pained loneliness, to nurse their grief. They may even become caustic to others.

But there is another way to look at adversity. Life is an education; and, if an education is to fulfill its function, there must be sharp discipline. Sorrow makes better people of those who look upon grief as discipline. They learn that with anguish there often comes illumination; with pain, purification; with suffering, a broadening of sympathies and understanding. Grief does not break such people. It makes them. It becomes a severe but a helpful teacher.

It ought to be clear to us that God does not promise to remove trouble. Rather he gives power to overcome it and to use it for great gain. The schoolboy who finds someone to do all his sums for him may think he is leading a happy life and getting the most out of it. But one day he will learn to his bitter disappointment that God did not intend that life should be so easy. He must work out the answer to his own problems, whether they be in the realm of arithmetic or sorrow. Grief bravely borne never destroys but always enriches the life of man. Hence comes peace and poise. Thus is true character built.

Have you ever watched a butterfly emerge from its chrysalis? If you have, you know the apparently painful struggle of the young wings to free themselves. Overcome by pity, a lad took up such a chrysalis and cut it open. The creature was freed, 'tis true, but be-

101

cause of the "kindness" it was foredoomed to go through life with undeveloped wing power. It could never soar to the heights, it could never enjoy life, as it could have done if its painful debut into this world had not been eased.

In like manner the man who does not have to struggle can never soar. Ease does not bring strength of character. The reverse is true, as Austin Phelps points out: "Suffering is a wonderful fertilizer to the roots of character. The great object of this life is character. This is the only thing we can carry with us into eternity. To gain the most of it and the best of it is the object of probation."

> Who never mourn'd hath never known
> What treasures grief reveals,
> The sympathies that humanize,
> The tenderness that heals,
>
> The power to look within the veil,
> And learn the heavenly lore,
> The keyword to life's mysteries
> So dark to us before.
>
> —Author unknown

33. *The Gift of Greatness*

⟨⟨∽⟩⟩

Life is not as idle ore,
But iron dug from central gloom,
    And heated hot with burning fears,
    And dipped in baths of hissing tears,
And batter'd with the shocks of doom
    To shape and use.

—Alfred Tennyson

There is a colorful fable of how birds first got their wings. One day God looked down and felt their form was not complete, their life too restricted. So he made soft-feathered wings and laid them before the wingless birds and said, "Come, take up these burdens and bear them."

But these tiny creatures were not quite sure they wanted the extra weight, the additional size. And so they did not immediately pick up the burdens which lay at their feet. But in time, one after another took them up in their beaks and laid them on their backs. For a while they staggered beneath the load. And then a strange thing happened. As these bundles of feathers were kept close over their hearts, they gradually grew fast. Soon the birds learned how to use them. No longer were their journeys limited to walking about the earth. The whole realm of the heavens

103

was theirs to explore. Their burdens had become wings.

Thus may our sorrow lift us into a realm of greatness which we could never have known without it. People nursed in ease and comfort, who know not the pang of suffering and sorrow, are prone to become soft-fibered and flabby. They can never be their greatest selves. Said a noted teacher to a talented singer, "If I could make you suffer for two years, you would be the greatest contralto in all Europe." The highest art springs from suffering.

The best in any man is called out by trying circumstances. This is one reason why age has so much more of mellowness and power than does youth. Remarked an Englishwoman about the first sermon she heard her minister preach, "Ah, 'twas very well, but it was almost all tinsel." Then this sainted man's wife died. The blow completely upset his world. It drove him to greater depths of thought. It tested his faith. And when he preached again, the same parishioner declared, "It is all gold now." So can your life be as that sermon, "all gold," if you accept the discipline of sorrow.

Think of the suffering of those who have achieved real greatness: Moses, who was not permitted to enter the Promised Land; Milton, blind and heartbroken. Could Dante have written as he did had Beatrice responded differently to his overtures? Schubert, who was never to know reciprocal love, poured out his passion in his *Unfinished Symphony*. Christ's apostles forsook him and fled. He died upon a cross.

Robert E. Lee philosophized on this truth:

How wide-lying and universal is the law of life! Where did the bravest man and purest woman you know get their whitened characters? Did they not get them as the clay gets its beauty—after the darkness and the burning of the furnace? Where did Savonarola get his eloquence? In the darkness and burning of the furnace wherein God discovered deep things to him. Where did Stradivari get his violins? Where did Titian get his color? Where did Angelo get his marbles? Where did Mozart get his music, and Chatterton his poetry, and Jeremiah his sermon?

They got them where the clay gets its glory and its shimmer—in the darkness and in the burning. Truly they can testify that God kept His promise who said, "I will give thee the treasures of darkness."

> Then, welcome each rebuff
> That turns earth's smoothness rough,
> Each sting that bids nor sit nor stand but go!
> Be our joy three-parts pain!
> Strive, and hold cheap the strain;
> Learn, nor account the pang; dare, never grudge
> the throe!

—ROBERT BROWNING

34. The Gift of Assurance

⟨∽∿∾⟩

Who ne'er his bread in sorrow ate,
  Who ne'er the mournful midnight hours
Weeping upon his bed has sate,
  He knows you not, ye Heavenly Powers.
                              —LONGFELLOW

We do not see the stars until the darkness falls. We cannot rightly evaluate life until we have tasted suffering. There are many things which keep people from thinking about God until some great shock forces them to face reality. He is more easily lost in the sunshine than in the storm. He is more easily found in sorrow than in joy.

Some people spend so much time in making a living that they never arrive at the business of making a life. But when sorrow comes they have to decide on a philosophy which makes room for suffering.

When everything is going smoothly one can truly enjoy material goods and intellectual pleasures, with his children around him and his family unbroken. But when one chair is left empty at the common board he is forced to seek more certain satisfactions.

Often we become so engrossed with the little concerns of everyday living that nothing less than the lightning and the thunder will cause us to lift our eyes heavenward to God!

Men live a superficial and shallow life because they have never given their existence serious thought. Plato says they live the unexamined life. The people who live for the world and its things—for pleasure or for wealth—have never really reasoned things out. But when sorrow comes life takes on a new color. True indeed are J. C. Lambert's words:

> Eyes which the preacher's art in vain hath schooled
>   By wayside graves are raised;
> And lips cry, God be merciful,
>   Which ne'er said, God be praised.

No less a one than Martin Luther's wife, religious though she was, declared after her husband's death, "I had never known what such and such things meant, in such and such psalms, such complaints and workings of spirit, I had never understood the practice of Christian duties, had not God brought me under some affliction."

The dew does not fall when the sun is shining. It is after the sun has gone down, when the cool breath of evening comes, when the dark curtains of the night have been drawn, that this benediction descends. So it is with our lives. It is when the light of life seems to have gone out that God reveals himself most intimately.

It is then we are forced to take the time to think about life, its meaning, its purpose. It is then that our own futility and inadequacy are laid bare and we are forced back upon God's purpose—there's just nowhere else to go. It is then that folly dies and one turns round to view life with sane and altered eyes. It is often in the vast silence which falls on the heart in grief that the voice of God is heard. In the strange play of opposites, we come to know and understand.

In Johan Bojer's *Great Hunger* Peer, who has given up the idea of God, loses his only and much-prized possession. The dog of an enemy neighbor kills his little child. In rebellious grief he cries out against the Eternal, against life, against himself, until he is half mad. And then comes light. In the deep stillness of the night he goes to a room where he proudly hoards a small amount of seed—only enough for his own little field. He takes half of it, and—well, hear his own words: "Therefore I went and sowed the corn in my enemy's field, that God might exist." Dante declared, "Sorrow remarries us to God." Peer found it so.

> I bless Thee, Lord, for sorrows sent
>   To break my dream of human power;
> For now, my shallow cisterns spent,
>   I find Thy founts, and thirst no more.
>
> I take Thy hand, and fears grow still;
>   Behold Thy face, and doubts remove;
> Who would not yield his wavering will
>   To perfect Truth and boundless Love?
>
> —Author unknown

35. *The Gift of Sympathy*

Grief halted at my door.
"My burden's great, and I'm footsore,"
Said he.
"Then, come thou in!"
I cried.
"The supper's spread—
The sweet rye bread."
Grief put his burden down,
And stepped inside,
And, parting, left a gift with me—
The world-wide gift of Sympathy.
                              —R. C. SHEFFIELD

We often speak of a feeling of sympathy *for* others, whereas it is really a feeling *with* others. He who has never known a deep sorrow may have a certain feeling toward another, but it cannot be compared to the real sympathy of the one who has suffered a like sorrow. Perhaps you have seen Domenichino's picture in which an angel is touching the points of the thorns in the Saviour's crown. The look in the eyes of that heavenly one is a look of wonder; not being human, the angel does not understand human suffering. Some people are like that angel. They cannot help another because, not having had the experience themselves, they do not understand.

Perhaps you are thinking of someone now. "He can't help me," you muse. "His life is in another sphere entirely." But no doubt there is another who has been of real help to you. "Yes," you reply, "because he has been through the mill." Grief gives us a common bond. We feel together and understand each other better. You, because of your trial, have come into possession of true sympathy. With Walt Whitman you can say, "Agonies are one of my changes of garments. I do not ask the wounded person how he feels. I myself become the wounded person. And whoever walks a furlong without sympathy, walks to his own funeral drest in his shroud."

Charles Kingsley was one day invited into the studio of the artist Turner to see one of the latter's paintings of a storm at sea. In wrapt admiration Kingsley gasped, "How did you do it, Turner?"

The painter replied: "I wished to paint a storm at sea, so I went to the coast of Holland, and engaged a fisherman to take me out in his boat in the next storm. The storm was brewing, and I went down to his boat and bade him tie me to its mast. Then he drove the boat out into the teeth of the storm. The storm was so furious that I longed to lie down in the bottom of the boat and allow it to blow over me. But I could not; I was bound to the mast. Not only did I see that storm and feel it, but it blew itself into me till I

110

became part of the storm. And then I came back and painted that picture."

It is after grief has blown itself into our very beings that we understand and appreciate the sorrowings of other people.

This possession of sympathy makes your life invaluable to your friends. You will be able to do for them in their hour of tragedy what many another cannot do. James Barrie saw this in his mother and he wrote: "She came back to her desolate home (after the death of her eldest son) and bowed herself before God. But she never recovered from the blow, from that time she sat in the chair by the window, tended by her noble daughter Jess. That is how my mother got her soft face . . . and her pathetic ways, and her large charities, and how other mothers ran to her when they had lost a child."

Then one ought to thank God for the sorrow which has come into his life. If he faces it rightly, it will give him far more than it takes from him. Just the gift of true sympathy is as priceless as rubies.

Concerning true sympathy Dr. J. H. Jowett wrote:

I do not think we shall ever have a really deep feeling for our fellow sufferers until we have deeply suffered too. You begin to pray for the sailors when your own boy is on the deep! When you have a crippled child what a heart you have for the maimed! The funeral procession in the street wears quite another appearance when one has

111

gone from your own doors! It sometimes seems as though God cannot draw us together in common feeling without taking us through a common sorrow. There is nothing that so welds hearts together as simultaneous passage through a common grief. Sundered brothers are bound together again at their mother's grave. I know of nothing more pathetic in the life of Browning than the reconciliation of himself and the great actor Macready. They had been close and intimate friends; but for some trifle or other they quarreled, and each went his own way, and for years their helpful intercourse was broken. Then came a great trouble. About the same time they lost their wives, and a little while after, as each was walking out his loneliness in a quiet way in a London suburb, they suddenly met face to face, and Browning, with a great burst of emotion, seized his old friend's hand and said, "Oh, Macready"; and Macready, with an aching heart replied, "Oh, Browning." That was all they could say to each other and in the fires of a great and common grief the two severed lives were welded again. God brings us together by common suffering. Our sympathy is born out of our sorrow, like fragrance from a crushed and beaten rose.

36. The Gift of Beauty

In the still air the music lies unheard;
   In the rough marble beauty hides unseen:
To wake the music and the beauty needs
   The master's touch, the sculptor's chisel keen.

THE GIFT OF BEAUTY

Great Master, touch us with thy skilful hand;
   Let not the music that is in us die!
Great Sculptor, hew and polish us; nor let
   Hidden and lost, thy form within us lie!

Spare not the stroke! do with us as thou wilt!
   Let there be naught unfinished, broken, marred;
Complete thy purpose, that we may become
   Thy perfect image, O our God and Lord!
                              —HORATIO BONAR

Beauty of life, like strength of character, is not born of ease. It comes from suffering. There may be a certain shallow attractiveness about the face which is perfect in every feature but which knows no care. If one wants to see genuine beauty, however, he will find it in the tender lines which sacrificial love has drawn upon a mother's face. The keen chisel hews out true beauty. The value of sorrow is not in what it takes from us as much as in what it fails to touch.

The story of the three men who went through the fiery furnace unscathed is of little use if we think of what the fire destroyed. The glory of the fiery furnace was its failure to touch the lives of these men. They came through untouched, unscorched. And their faces shone with an inner glory. Just so may one who undergoes sorrow come through the experience with far more beauty of character than he entered it.

Not only will our sorrow add new beauty to our

113

lives, it will shed new beauty upon the life of our loved one. How easy it is now to forget all the unpleasant things! We want, and rightly too, to remember only the good. Right now you appreciate the one who is gone far more than you did before.

In a scintillating novel a stern old mother had a daughter who was given to writing. The elder one disapproved of this tendency and gustily called the girl's accomplishments "verses." Then her child was taken from her and she always referred to them thereafter as "poems." Indeed, sorrow transfigures everything and makes it stand out in a new light. Perhaps we could not see all the good qualities and worthfulness of our dear one while he was with us, but they stand out now with startling clearness.

> 'Tis only when they spring to heaven that angels
> Reveal themselves to you; they sit all day
> Beside you, and lie down at night by you
> Who care not for their presence, muse or sleep.
> And all at once they leave you, and you know them!
>
> ROBERT BROWNING

Out of suffering comes victory. Death is the forerunner of life. In Holman Hunt's "The Light of the World" this truth is portrayed in the crown of thorns upon the Master's head. Every prong has sent forth a shoot of greenery. The thorns have blossomed.

There is a legend which tells how some monks, long

ago, found the crown of thorns which the Saviour had worn. With great reverence they took it and placed it on the altar in the chancel of their chapel. On Easter morn one of the monks entered the chapel early. The room was filled with a fragrant perfume. He could not understand it. When he came to the altar, a crown still lay there. But it was no longer a crown of thorns—but of beautiful roses! Thus sorrow may blossom as a rose.

37. The Gift of Joy

Weeping may tarry for the night,
But joy cometh in the morning.
—Psalm 30:5

It is difficult, in the dark night of sorrow, to realize that the sun is sure to shine again, that our voices will be lifted in song again, that our weeping will be turned into joy. But this is the promise which we as believers in the all-wise God are given. Light always follows darkness. The night may appear very black, but the day dawns with a ray of hope. Then let us not judge the future during the hour of our darkest grief. Rather let us patiently endure, knowing that a new joy eventually will be ours.

An interesting story is told of Sadu Sundar Singh. He was driven from a village in India where he had been preaching the gospel. Having no place else to go, he sought refuge in a near-by cave, where he prepared to spend the night. Suddenly he was surrounded by a group of armed men. He thought there would be nothing to do but surrender. He knelt in prayer for some minutes, and when he opened his eyes the men were gone. He then lay down and went to sleep. When he awoke in the morning, the same men were all around him. Ready to give himself up, he approached their leader, who said: "We have not come this morning to do you any harm, but to ask you who was with you last evening. We had indeed intended to kill you, but you had so many people around you that we could not get at you." For Sadu Sundar Singh, the very danger of death itself had fled with the night. He was safe. Thus is it with our grief. When its night is upon us our sorrow may seem to be more than we can bear. Then the beauty of God's morning light drives away our care and replaces it with joy.

Why can we be assured that joy will come with the morning? Is it not because we can be masters over all situations? This is the Christian belief. And with the knowledge that we are masters there comes a sense of joy and calm.

> When thou comest to the waters
> Thou shalt not go down, but through.
>
> —ANNIE J. PLINT

Again, if we meet our sorrow rightly, we can be assured of joy because of the real happiness which accomplishment brings. In prospect we may believe we are masters. In actual experience we learn that we are. Said a lady who was dying of cancer: "If I had been told six months ago that I should be able to bear so much suffering, I should never have believed it. But I have borne it, and believe I can bear more. This very thought is a source of inner joy." It is always a joy to accomplish something. To meet grief triumphantly brings the joy of accomplishment.

True and deep joy comes as a result of genuine understanding. And true understanding comes only with experience. The child whose parent takes it on a vacation may be filled with a certain glee. But it does not know such deep joy as the parent experiences; for the latter knows what sacrifices had to be made for this vacation, and what such a period of rest and play can do to rebuild the physical and the mental powers. After sorrow has visited a person he understands life much better; he appreciates it far more. His joy is more stable, more powerful, more complete. With deep insight George Matheson wrote:

> O joy that seekest me through pain,
> I cannot close my heart to Thee;
> I trace the rainbow through the rain,
> And feel the promise is not vain
> That morn shall tearless be.

A FINAL WORD

38. Time Heals

◈

"Time brings roses," declares an ancient proverb. They cannot be grown overnight. Slowly a bush unfolds its leaves. Then a bud appears, and finally the rose in full bloom. One does not try to hurry nature.

Comfort in sorrow is like a rose. It does not come quickly. Our wound heals only gradually. It is foolish to demand an immediate release from our empty loneliness. Entreating hands must fold themselves and wait. God will not fail us. He sends time to be our healing minister.

Much of our grief is due to our impatience. The more accustomed we are to having our wishes fulfilled at once, the more efficient we are in accomplishing huge tasks, the more difficult it will be for us to permit time to pursue its magic course. We may feel that God should send angels down to open the grave and restore our loved one. In our impatience we fail to appreciate that the days and months come as angels with healing in their wings.

Who has not seen a field of unsightly dead cornstalks transformed by the quiet falling of crystal snow

into a fairy forest of white? So time quietly and un-
obtrusively drops moment after moment into the scar
of our grief until it is covered and transformed. James
Russell Lowell has beautifully expressed this thought:

> I stood and watched by the window
>   The noiseless work of the sky,
> And the sudden flurries of snow-birds,
>   Like brown leaves whirling by.
>
> I thought of a mound in Sweet Auburn
>   Where a little headstone stood;
> How the flakes were folding it gently,
>   As did robins the babes in the woods.
>
> Up spoke our own little Mable
>   Saying, "Father, who makes it snow?"
> And I told of the good All-father
>   Who cares for us here below.
>
> Again I looked at the snow-fall,
>   And thought of the leaden sky
> That arched o'er our first great sorrow,
>   When that mound was heaped so high.
>
> I remembered that gradual patience
>   That fell from that cloud like snow,
> Flake by flake, healing and hiding
>   The scar that renewed our woe.

And again to the child I whispered,
   "The snow that husheth all,
Darling, the merciful Father
   Alone can make it fall!"

Look about you. Your friends have suffered, too.
Their grief was once as blinding as yours is now.
Lovingly they are trying to impart what reason can
never convey. Time, like an ever-moving stream, has
borne their grief away. As sadness and loneliness now
seem to clutch at your throat, know that time will
likewise be very good to you. Be assured that this
experience, however deeply it has pierced your heart,
will pass away; that where now there is darkness
there will soon be light; that the cloud will pass and
the sun once more will shed its radiance upon you.

Once in Persia reigned a king
Who upon his signet ring
Graved a maxim true and wise,
Which, if held before the eyes,
Gave him counsel at a glance,
Fit for every change and chance.
Solemn words, and these are they:
"Even this shall pass away."

Trains of camels through the sand
Brought him gems from Samarcand;
Fleets of galleys through the seas
Brought him pearls to match with these.

But he counted not his gain
Treasures of the mine or main;
"What is wealth?" the king would **say;**
"Even this shall pass away."

In the revels of his court
At the zenith of the sport,
When the palms of all his guests
Burned with clapping at his jests;
He amid his figs and wine,
Cried: "Oh, loving friends of mine!
Pleasure comes but not to stay;
Even this shall pass away."

Fighting on a furious field,
Once a javelin pierced his shield;
Soldiers with a loud lament
Bore him bleeding to his tent;
Groaning from his tortured side,
"Pain is hard to bear," he cried,
"But with patience, day by day,—
Even this shall pass away."

Towering in the public square,
Twenty cubits in the air,
Rose his statue, carved in stone,
Then the king, disguised, unknown,
Stood before his sculptured name
Musing meekly, "What is fame?
Fame is but a slow decay—
Even this shall pass away."

121

FROM SUNSET TO DAWN

Struck with palsy, sere and old,
Waiting at the gates of gold,
Said he with his dying breath:
"Life is done, but what is death?"
Then, in answer to the king,
Fell a sunbeam on his ring,
Showing by a heavenly ray,
"Even this shall pass away."

—THEODORE TILTON

Acknowledgments

Gratitude is here expressed to authors, publishers, and other copyright owners who have graciously granted permission for reproduction of their material in this book. Every effort has been made to discover the authorship and ownership of each selection used. If there has been any error or oversight, apologies are offered and correction will be made in subsequent printings.

Specific acknowledgment is made to the following publishers:

ABINGDON-COKESBURY PRESS for nine lines of poetry from *Christ at the Round Table* by E. Stanley Jones, copyright 1928.

THE BEACON PRESS, Boston, Massachusetts, for two stanzas of "Thy Brother" by Theodore C. Williams, from *Hymns of the Spirit.*

THE BOBBS-MERRILL COMPANY for the poem "Away" by James Whitcomb Riley, copyright 1907.

W. B. CONKEY COMPANY for "And So for Me" from *Collected Poems of Ella Wheeler Wilcox,* copyright 1920.

DODD, MEAD & COMPANY, INC., for five lines of "When All Is Done" from *Complete Poems* of Paul Laurence Dunbar, copyright 1913; for two lines of *Hound of*

124

NOBLE AND NOBLE PUBLISHERS, INC., for the poem "Don't Let the Song Go Out of Your Life" from *The Bright Side* by Kate Stiles. Used by special permission of the publishers.

CHARLES SCRIBNER'S SONS for "If All the Skies" from *Poems of Henry van Dyke,* copyright 1911.

WARD LOCK & COMPANY, LTD., for a poem from *Through the Windows of a Little House* by Fay Inchfawn, copyright 1933.

Specific acknowledgment is made to the following authors and heirs of authors:

CHARLES K. BOLTON for the poem "The Inevitable" by his mother, Sarah K. Bolton.

MRS. ROBERT FREEMAN for the poem "The Other Room" by her husband, Robert Freeman.

STRICKLAND GILLILAN for the poem "The Lord Giveth."